PSYCHOACTIVE DRUG USE IN SPORT

THEORY, RESEARCH, AND POLICY

PSYCHOACTIVE DRUG USE IN SPORT

THEORY, RESEARCH, AND POLICY

KATHERINE MCLEAN

A link to access additional online resources is provided at:
https://doi.org/10.18848/978-1-963049-21-3/CGP

SPORT & SOCIETY POCKETBOOK TEACHING SERIES

The **Sport and Society Pocketbook Teaching Series** aims to introduce students and a general readership to relevant topics, theories, and concepts within sport history and sport sociology. The topics will vary but are united in their purpose to serve as an accessible alternative to generic textbook offerings or academic research monographs. We hope that the shorter and more accessible pocketbook format of the series will mean that each book can be read in an hour or two on a quiet evening or while commuting on a bus or train. This aligns with our ethos of accessibility in scholarly communication.

Books in the series can be accessed in print and electronic formats. In addition, and in parallel to both editions, each title will be accompanied by an online repository where additional learning and teaching resources are provided. The electronic platform for the series will include links to recent and significant research articles, visual materials, podcasts, lectures, and more, thus securing ongoing relevance by providing new and engaging resources and perspectives aligned with the topic of each book.

This series is for teachers, learners, and individuals with an interest in sports alike.

Dr. Jörg Krieger (Aarhus University, Denmark)
Dr. April Henning (Heriot-Watt University, United Kingdom)
Dr. Lindsay Parks Pieper (University of Lynchburg, United States)
Dr. Jesper Andreasson (Linnaeus University, Sweden)

First published in 2024
as part of the Sport and Society Book Imprint
doi: 10.18848/978-1-963049-21-3/CGP (Full Book)

Common Ground Research Networks
2001 South First St, Suite 201L
University of Illinois Research Park
Champaign, IL
61820

Copyright © McLean, Katherine 2024

All rights reserved. Apart from fair dealing for the purposes of study, research, criticism or review as permitted under the applicable copyright legislation, no part of this book may be reproduced by any process without written permission from the publisher.

Library of Congress Cataloging-in-Publication Data

Names: McLean, Katherine, author.
Title: Psychoactive drug use in sport : theory, research, and policy / Katherine McLean.
Description: Champaign, IL : Common Ground Research Networks, [2024] | Includes bibliographical references. | Summary: "This book presents a broad epidemiological portrait of psychoactive drug use among athletes, bolstered by a sociological framework that problematizes sport as a "risk environment" for substance use. Interventions, policy options, and sporting contexts that may reduce or minimize drug-related harms, or encourage controlled substance use, are considered throughout the text. In addition to sketching a global history of psychoactive drug use in sport, two drug-specific case studies are presented in detail: alcohol use and overuse among university and non-elite "club" athletes, and the non-medical consumption of opioids within contact sports. An interdisciplinary text, this book provides a comprehensive review of current research in psychoactive drug use in sport, as well as a guide to evidence-based interventions"-- Provided by publisher.
Identifiers: LCCN 2024004362 (print) | LCCN 2024004363 (ebook) | ISBN 9781963049190 (paperback) | ISBN 9781963049213 (pdf) | ISBN 9781963049206 (epub)
Subjects: LCSH: Athletes--Drug use. | Athletes--Substance use. | Psychotropic drugs--Physiological effect. | Sports--Psychological aspects.
Classification: LCC RC1230 .M378 2024 (print) | LCC RC1230 (ebook) | DDC

Cover Image: Peter Hermes Furian (Shutterstock)

TABLE OF CONTENTS

Introduction 1

Epidemiology and History of Drug Use in Sport 21

Theories of Psychoactive Substance Use in Sport 55

Alcohol Use and Sport 91

Opioid Use and Sport 125

Conclusion 161

CHAPTER 1

Introduction

Key Concepts and Definitions

This book is focused on the use of psychoactive substances by self-identified athletes, and/or within sport and fitness contexts. Not to be confused with the more specific categories of "psychedelic" or "*new* psychoactive substances," a **psychoactive substance** is one that affects the brain, often causing changes in mood, awareness, thoughts, feelings, or behavior (Kuhn et al., 2019). Preceded by the "psychoactive" label, the terms "substance" and "drug" will be used interchangeably throughout this text, although the latter—heavy with cultural and historical baggage—is deserving of explicit explanation. A **drug** is simply any chemical compound that impacts one's mental or bodily functions, a definition that encompasses a vast array of substances, from aspirin, to alcohol, and, perhaps, sugar (Kuhn et al., 2019). While a growing research corpus confirms that sugars activate the same neurochemical pathways as well-known intoxicants like cocaine, we will not consider foods as relevant psychoactive substances in this book (although, given the simultaneous improvements in athletic performance and nutritional access over the 20th century, other authors might critically assess the status of food as a performance-enhancing drug!)

Given the foregoing definition of "psychoactive substances," pharmaceuticals that primarily affect physical function, without impacting mental state, will not prominently figure in the chapters to come. We will, however, identify and discuss athletes' substance use without undue attention to motivation; indeed, the designation of "psychoactive" is preferred for its pertinence to a number of **drug use** patterns and preferences, particularly in the realm of sport. Psychoactive substances may be ingested to achieve pleasure, ameliorate pain, calm the mind, or energize the body—or any combination of these ends; they may also be consumed for no specific or premeditated reason at all. In the words of the renowned sociologist Howard S. Becker, the "motivation or disposition to engage in [marijuana use] is built up in the course of learning to engage in it, and does not antedate this learning process" (1953, p. 235). Certain analgesics or "painkillers," prevalent in sport, possess potent euphoric properties for novice users, a quality that further complicates the assessment of motives for use over time; individuals' motives for such substance use might not only change but may also be multiple, conflicted, and not entirely aligned with the drugs' physical and mental effects. Overall, athletes engage in numerous patterns of drug use classified by motive, all of which may involve psychoactive drugs.

In light of this complexity, this book will not refer to "recreational" drug use, a classification that implies sociality, pleasure, and/or consumption for casual purposes. Moreover, the "recreational" label is laden with negative connotations within societal contexts of drug **prohibition**, where drug use for pleasure may be framed as unnecessary, frivolous, selfish, or dangerous. This qualification is rarely applied to the use of licit (if regulated) psychoactive drugs such as alcohol or tobacco, two substances that are commonly consumed by certain subsets of athletes and whose use will be discussed in depth. Psychoactive substances span the legal/illegal divide—another reason for employing this term to define the scope of this text. Finally, the book follows Craig Reinarman's (1994, p. 161) maxim that "drugs are inanimate objects without social consequence until they are ingested by humans," a description that belies the notion that any substance—licit or illicit—is inherently prone to harmful patterns of use. Accordingly, stigmatizing and imprecise terms such as "drugs of abuse" will be avoided throughout. Indeed, a guiding assumption of this text is that all psychoactive substance may be used in ways that do not necessarily harm the individual consumer or the community that surrounds them; we will be particularly interested in how sport settings and subcultures serve to modulate the risks and benefits associated with any kind of drug use.

Of course, some individuals may suffer physiological, psychological, and social harms as a consequence of their psychoactive substance use, a reality that will not be ignored but rather put into context. It might here also be put in perspective in noting that national survey data reveals most people's consumption of psychoactive drugs to be limited in time, sporadic, and noncompulsive (European Monitoring Centre for Drugs and Drug Addiction [EMCDDA], 2022; U.S. Department of Health and Human Services, Substance Abuse and Mental Health Services Administration, Center for Behavioral Health Statistics and Quality, 2020). In light of this evidence, we will default to the description of drug consumption as drug "use," not abuse; in fact, the latter term, as well as other morally loaded and vague concepts such as "addiction," will be eschewed overall. Prescription drug consumption that exceeds medically recommended dosage or frequency of administration or that is intended to produce euphoria is commonly characterized as "misuse"; however, this book prefers to speak of the **"nonmedical"** use of prescribed drugs, when talking about individuals who consume such drugs outside of medical supervision.

Lastly, patterns of psychoactive substance use that results in loss of control, physiological or social impairment, and psychological distress will be identified as **substance use disorders** (SUDs), a term first formalized by the fifth edition of *Diagnostic and Statistical Manual of Mental Disorders* (*DSM-5*) (American Psychiatric Association, 2013). While we will not dwell on the 11 diagnostic criteria stipulated by the *DSM-5*, the label of "substance use disorder" is chosen for its relative precision in definition and its broad conceptualization of medical, mental, and social harms. It should be noted that the *DSM-5* categorization of SUD includes manifestations of physical dependence, namely, **tolerance** ("a markedly diminished effect with continued use of the same amount of [a] substance") and **withdrawal** (physiological distress associated with the cessation of substance use). The development of drug dependence may play an important role in mediating athletes' substance use trajectories; in fact, both substance classes discussed in the books concluding case studies are associated with clinically significant tolerance and withdrawal symptoms. At the same time, not all drugs produce (physical) dependence, and so the latter term should not be read as synonymous with SUD.

While not the focus of this text, it may be prudent to also define **image and performance-enhancing drugs (IPED)** and "doping," given the fuzzy boundaries that separate IPED from the psychoactive substances that form the subject of this work. Indeed, this is a very delicate demarcation, in light of the fact that IPED are often defined in policy terms, as "substances banned by the World Anti-Doping Agency (WADA)"—a grouping that includes many psychoactive drugs (UK Anti-Doping [UKAD], n.d.). (As a general introduction to psychoactive substance use in sport and fitness contexts, this book prefers "image and performance-enhancing drugs," or IPED, to the slimmer designation of "performance-enhancing drugs," or IPED. The former term allows for a broader application to gym-going or bodybuilding populations who seek to change their appearance through the use of legal and banned substances [EMCDDA, 2021].) The consumption of IPED in the context of (elite) sport is one form of "**doping**," a practice that is itself legally constituted and elliptically defined as any "violation of one of the anti-doping rules laid out in the World Anti-Doping Code" (Henning et al., 2021). Reviewing such language, it is immediately clear that psychoactive and IPED use may be *legally* indistinguishable among athletes under the surveillance of international, national, or institutional antidoping authorities. Indeed, antidoping authorities assume a "strict liability" approach to individuals who test positive for prohibited substances, whether or not they have psychoactive properties. In order to avoid sanctioning, athletes must be granted a **therapeutic use exemption (TUE)**, or formal recognition of medical need for certain drug treatments, requiring the testimony of a health-care provider. In this way, "medical use" of banned substances reflects institutional or legal recognition as much as an individual athlete's motivation.

When taking a "careers" or longitudinal perspective on individual athletes' substance use, it is also difficult to theoretically disentangle the use of a drug for performance or other purposes, another reason why this book remains agnostic on motive. Among pharmacologists and sociologists alike, it is widely recognized that a drugs' effects are shaped by intention and setting; the psychoactive effects of a drug ingested to boost physical agility may be little noticed, while a substance consumed to induce sedation or relieve anxiety may have an inadvertent impact on sports performance (Zinberg, 1986). Recognizing these fluid distinctions, this book will remain open to the discussion of IPED among athletes as they intersect with the use of psychoactive substances in this population. Similarly, it will discuss the use of legal substances that are prohibited by neither national laws nor antidoping organizations, yet may have measurable impacts on athletes' health, image, performance, and overarching well-being.

Psychoactive Substance Use Among Athletes: A New Problem?

The spectacle of illicit or otherwise banned substance use (i.e., doping) among high-profile athletes has become a staple feature of news outlets worldwide. Beyond carrying implications for competition results, titles, and sport-specific records, such cases may be read as compelling morality tales—stories of once admired athletes falling prey to their own anxieties, ego, or thirst for success. Indeed, U.S. cycling star Lance Armstrong's confessed involvement in a multiyear doping scheme that spanned his seven Tour de France titles was among the biggest news stories of 2013; more recently, revelations of a state-sponsored doping program among elite Russian athletes has consumed international media outlets with the arrival of every Olympic event since 2016 (Ingle, 2013; Klosok, n.d.). News coverage around such scandals has likely both responded to, and fed, public perception of a global doping crisis. A 2014 Harris Poll of U.S. adults found that over half identified "cheating in sport as the greatest offense that can be done by an Olympic athlete or team"; 89% of participants agreed that "more action needs to be taken to prevent the use of performance-enhancing drugs" among professional and Olympic athletes (n.a., 2014).

While the narratives of many fallen sports idols revolve around their consumption of IPED, prominent athletes' use of psychoactive substances, not necessarily known for conferring

an athletic advantage, is also a site of significant social concern—
albeit one animated by different interests. Athletes suspected of
doping, or IPED use, are often spurned for seeking "superhuman"
status; by contrast, those linked with illegal or recreational drug
misuse may be seen as succumbing to all-too-human pressures, an
understanding associated with both sympathy and stigmatization.
Professional athletes' drug involvement may be read as indicative
of the vast scope of an ongoing drug problem, a signal that no one
is truly immune to the lure of inherently dangerous substances.
National Hockey League (NHL) "enforcer" Derek Boogard's
2011 death from alcohol and OxyContin toxicity solidified
recognition of the mounting opioid and overdose crises in the
United States, even as rates of opioid dependence and related
mortality had been rising for over a decade (Munson, 2013).
Moreover, the tragic death of a celebrity athlete might serve as
the crucial tinder needed to ignite a sweeping drug scare, a fact
demonstrated by the federal Len Bias Law criminalizing fatal
drug delivery, named after a rising basketball star who died from
a cocaine-induced heart attack in 1986 (Gelber, 2021).

Whether or not such drug use is in the service of sports performance, there is little evidence that athletes' consumption of
controlled substances has increased over time or represents a new
problem. Indeed, the intentional ingestion of stimulants by endurance athletes was both recorded, and revered, in the 19th century,
before being targeted by the antidrug campaigns of the Progressive era (see Dimeo, 2007 for an in-depth history of stimulant
use in sport.) What little data exists on the use of psychoactive
substances among elite and amateur athletes points to a general
decline over recent decades, a drop that mirrors ebbing rates of
drug use in the general population. Still, this overarching trend
obscures a more complex reality with regard to psychoactive
substance use in sport—a phenomenon, it should be said, that

is hard to sharply delineate from athletes' consumption of IPED. The gradual "mainstreaming" of medicinal cannabis has obvious implications for athletes' use of the drug as an analgesic, which is further abetted by the liberalization of marijuana prohibitions at both the state, and competition or league, level. At the end of 2021, over 80% of U.S. professional sports teams played within states that had partially or fully legalized marijuana; globally, at least 35 nations permit medical or recreational cannabis, although all cannabinoids, with the exception of cannabidiol, remain on the World Anti-Doping Association's in-competition "Prohibited List" (Kaplan, 2020; WADA, 2022). It is undoubtedly difficult to distinguish athletes' consumption of cannabis for therapeutic or sedative purposes, but use of the drug may be growing alongside increased acceptance of its pain management properties—and increasing recognition of the harms associated with prescription opioids (POs). Indeed, some research has identified sports injury and related surgeries as risk factors for opioid exposure and misuse (Ford et al., 2018). While it is not clear that athletes are more likely to develop opioid use disorders, the perception of this problem has shaped substance use policies in both sport and society at large.

The Big Picture: Athlete Drug Use in Context

Psychoactive substance use—and associated public concern—represent seemingly inescapable facets of social life in the 21st century. Yet the intentional pursuit of an altered consciousness through the consumption of certain chemicals (and/or their plant substrates) is widely recognized as a fundamental human behavior and a "social fact" that has characterized every documented civilization (Courtwright, 2002; Durkheim, 1982). Indeed, it is likely that individuals in many premodern societies boasted much higher levels of psychoactive substance or "drug" use than those seen today, as necessary means of getting nutrition, treating infectious disease, and managing pain before the advent of industrialized agriculture, specific medications, and anesthetics. Of course, many motivations for substance use are arguably trans-historical and thus familiar: to experience pleasure, alleviate boredom, promote creativity, and forge personal and community connections through social ritual.

While psychoactive substance use is arguably not unique to, or even emblematic of, highly developed societies, late modernity has facilitated novel types, methods, and patterns of consumption—a side effect of globalization, and the increase in international economic, interpersonal, scientific, and cultural exchange occasioned thereby. Substances that were once confined to the microclimates that supported their growth—for example, the mild-psychedelic plant, kratom—have experienced a surge in international popularity, alongside the growth of a digitally connected consumer base. Where the whole leaves of the kratom tree have been chewed, smoked, or steeped for millennia in Southeast Asia, technological developments have allowed for the infusion of their psychoactive components into tablets, capsules, or extracts (Cinosi et al., 2015; U.S. Drug Enforcement Administration [USDEA], 2020). Recent political and public health events of multinational import have also shaped the **epidemiology** of drug use in large parts of the world. For example, many countries within the Global North have struggled to contain rising levels of opioid (e.g., heroin, oxycodone, fentanyl) used misuse in the 21st century, a geographically dispersed problem with diverse causes: international and civil conflicts from Afghanistan to Colombia have encouraged the expansion of opium production within places hosting few other income-generating options; at the same time, major pharmaceutical companies have developed potent new opioid-type drugs, mass-marketed to aging and injury-prone populations living within consumer-driven health-care systems.

The so-called opioid epidemic exemplifies several trends within the current landscape of psychoactive substance use—the synergistic relationship between different substances, the fluid boundaries separating "medicine" from "drug," and the role of technological innovations in creating new consumers. It must be acknowledged that patterns of drug use tend to be highly localized, reflecting very specific social contexts, but the handful of psychoactive substances experiencing global surges in popularity do indeed fit the foregoing criteria (Ritchie & Roser, 2018). In the past decade, the use of two potent stimulants—cocaine and methamphetamine—has risen from North America to Southeast Asia, as individuals seek substances that are complementary to opioids and exploit new means of manufacture that have reduced retail prices. Several countries that have recently legalized medical and/or recreational cannabis have, in turn, witnessed a steady uptick in the adult prevalence of cannabis consumption, with some allowing the former drug in the treatment of opioid dependence (Haffajee & Mauri, 2021; Hasin & Walsh, 2021). Finally, "vapes" and other electronic nicotine delivery systems (ENDS) have followed a complicated trajectory in the places that permit them: first adopted by existing tobacco users, vaping has quickly gained traction among adolescents and young adults who had never smoked cigarettes; even as vaping has eclipsed smoking within this population, young people who vape demonstrate significantly higher rates of cigarette initiation (Al-Hamdani & Manly, 2021).

Such recent trends within drug use do not necessarily imply the emergence of new "drug problems" whether on a global or local scale. Not only are sweeping increases in opioid, stimulant, cannabis, and ENDS consumption associated with vastly different (and context contingent) individual and social harms, but, further, "drug problems" represent socially negotiated constructs, both tied to, but independent of, actual types and levels of drug use in a given place. Moreover, to paraphrase Craig Reinarman's (1994) classic work on "drug scares," societal attention to substance use is often reflective of the identity of those who use, not the substances they consume. Such attention may accrue to groups of relatively high or low social status, following impulses to help or control, empathize or stigmatize; the framing of different drug problems also exposes specific cultural understandings of drug use, its morality and risks, within different populations, as defined by race, class, gender, age—or occupation. This book considers the specific relationship between psychoactive substance use and sport, a topic of keen interest to policymakers, professional stakeholders, the global mediascape, and the general public. Through a review of empirical evidence and relevant sociological theories, it will consider whether such interest is warranted, and why; it will additionally ask how the prohibition and surveillance of certain kinds of psychoactive substance use among athletes shapes or exacerbates the very "problems" such interventions are intended to solve.

Road Map for the Book

The remaining text will seek to paint a broad epidemiological portrait of psychoactive drug use among athletes, bolstered by a theoretical framework that highlights salient sociological features of sport and the social psychology of athletic teams and competition. To introduce an influential heuristic early on, we will analyze sport—writ large and small—as a **"risk environment"** for drug use, which serves to modulate not only the likelihood of psychoactive substance use but also the associated harms (Rhodes, 2009). Conversely, the protective effects of sport participation will be considered, as will interventions or policy suites that might construct "enabling environments," or sporting contexts in which psychoactive drug use is controlled and diverse risks are minimized (Henning et al., 2021). In illustrating not only the "risk environment" but also other explanatory constructs, two drug-specific case studies will be presented in some detail: alcohol use and overuse among university and nonelite "club" athletes and the nonmedical consumption of opioids within contact sports. Both types and patterns of drug use will be resituated within a general population and policy landscape in conclusion. A more in-depth road map of the chapters to come follows.

Synthesizing available scholarly and governmental data, Chapter 2 will present an overview of contemporary and historical trends in psychoactive substance use in sport, providing comparative statistics on drug use among nonathletes where possible. We will also identify social, demographic, and sports-specific risk factors for drug use as documented within extant research, further describing their confluence or synergies (e.g., the ways in which masculine norms around risk-taking are amplified among those enacting a "toxic jock identity"— see Miller et al., 2006). This chapter will also consider ways in which drug prohibitions in sport have not only responded to but also (arguably) produced patterns of harmful substance use among athletes. In contemplating how tenuously evidenced certain substance bans are, Chapter 2 will also introduce a conflict theory of drug use and policy, namely, Craig Reinarman's (1994) "drug scares." In turn, Chapter 3 will review a series of empirically tested theories of psychoactive drug use in sport. While many such theories represent adaptations or applications of more general theories of drug use and deviance, extant research has also identified some drug use careers that are uniquely prevalent within sport, such as medical use pathways or polypharmacy combining IPED with psychoactive substances.

Having established both substance use trends and ways of understanding them, Chapters 4 and 5 will present two case studies of psychoactive drug use in sport. Beyond exploring two purported "problem substances" for athletes, these case studies also illustrate two of this text's overarching themes, namely, that substance use among athletes generally mirrors larger population trends, which the sport context may sometimes amplify and exacerbate. Chapter 4 will examine the use of alcohol among athletes, with a focus on the sporting social contexts that have been shown to promote binge and heavy drinking, particularly among university athletes and nonelite or "club" athletes. In drawing out specific sport risk environments for alcohol use, this chapter will also seek to sketch their inverse: sport and team cultures that enable moderate levels of drinking or alternative forms of sociality. An illicit drug case study, Chapter 5 will critically consider the incidence of opioid use disorders among athletes, contrasting popular representations of a "hidden epidemic" among athletes with an emerging literature showing a much more circumscribed problem within a handful of sports. Beyond exploring the possible harms associated with opioid use among athletes, this chapter will consider how societal anxieties and growing prohibitions around opioids at large may encourage equally risky pain management practices among athletes—and others. Both case studies will review evidence-based interventions for the prevention, treatment, and harm reduction of alcohol and opioid use disorders among athletes. As the world spirals to new peaks of alcohol overuse and opioid-related overdose in the wake of the COVID-19 pandemic, we will also question the relevance of athlete-specific interventions to a wider public.

Chapter 6, the final chapter, will revisit the musings of this introduction, in considering how sporting contexts represent a microcosm of broader substance use patterns within society at large. Here we will offer both "major takeaways" from the text, as well as questions for further reflection and directions for new research on drug use in sport.

Reflection Points

1. How might sporting contexts and careers promote or protect against psychoactive substance use and related use disorders?

2. What kind of "problem" is psychoactive substance use in sport? What social and historical factors have led to the problematization of this phenomenon?

3. How are the use of psychoactive and IPED connected? How useful are these distinctions, and how distinct are these two categories? How do these classifications reflect different cultural and historical framings of sport?

Glossary

Doping: Legally, violation of one of the antidoping rules laid out in the World Anti-Doping Code; colloquially, consumption of a banned substance or participation in a banned practice with the intention of improving performance within an athletic, skill-, or appearance-based competition.

Drug: Any chemical compound that impacts one's mental or bodily functions, a definition that encompasses a vast array of substances, from aspirin, to alcohol, and, perhaps, sugar.

Drug Use: A term describing consumption of chemical compounds without implying negative consequences or specific motivations.

Epidemiology: The study of the distribution of health conditions and related behaviors. Epidemiology identifies particular populations that are at higher risk for negative health outcomes, due to certain physical, social, or behavioral exposures.

Image and Performance-Enhancing Drugs (IPED): Legally, any substance banned by the World Anti-Doping Agency (WADA); colloquially, any substance that is used to improve performance within an athletic, skill-, or appearance-based competition.

Nonmedical Use: The consumption of any substance outside of, or in contradiction to, medical guidance. In practice, nonmedical drug use may involve consuming more of a substance than prescribed; consuming a substance more frequently than prescribed; consuming a prescribed substance for the purpose of intoxication; or consuming a controlled substance that was not prescribed.

Prohibition: A legal or policy regime that seeks to ban and sanction the consumption of certain substances.

Psychoactive Substance: A chemical compound that affects the brain, often causing changes in mood, awareness, thoughts, feelings, or behavior.

Risk Environment: A theoretical framework that shows how drug-related risk is shaped by an individual's physical, social, economic, and policy contexts.

Substance Use Disorder: A pattern of psychoactive substance use that results in loss of control, physiological or social impairment, and psychological distress.

Therapeutic Use Exemption (TUE): The formal permission of an antidoping organization, granted to an applicant athlete, to use a banned substance or technique in order to treat a diagnosed medical problem. While applying to the medical use of certain drugs, a TUE is a legal or institutional designation.

Tolerance: A biological phenomena that occurs after regular use of different psychoactive substances, characterized by a markedly diminished effect when using the same amount of [a] substance.

Withdrawal: A state of physiological distress associated with the cessation of substance use.

REFERENCES

Al-Hamdani, M., & Manly, E. (2021). Smoking cessation or initiation: The paradox of vaping. *Preventive Medicine Reports*, *22*, 101363. https://doi.org/10.1016/j.pmedr.2021.101363

American Psychiatric Association. (2013). *Diagnostic and statistical manual of mental disorders* (5th ed.).

Becker, H. S. (1953). Becoming a Marihuana user. *American Journal of Sociology*, *59*(3), 235–242. https://doi.org/10.1086/221326

Cinosi, E., Martinotti, G., Simonato, P., Singh, D., Demetrovics, Z., Roman-Urrestarazu, A., Bersani, F. S., Vicknasingam, B., Piazzon, G., Li, J.-H., Yu, W.-J., Kapitány-Fövény, M., Farkas, J., Di Giannantonio, M., & Corazza, O. (2015). Following "the roots" of Kratom (*Mitragyna speciosa*): The evolution of an enhancer from a traditional use to increase work and productivity in Southeast Asia to a recreational psychoactive drug in Western Countries. *BioMed Research International*, *2015*, 968786. https://doi.org/10.1155/2015/968786

Courtwright, D. (2002). *Forces of habit: Drugs and the making of the modern world*. Harvard University Press.

Dimeo, P. (2007). *A history of drug use in sport 1876–1976: Beyond good and evil*. Routledge.

Durkheim, E. (1982). *Rules of the sociological method* (2nd ed.). Free Press.

European Monitoring Centre for Drugs and Drug Addiction. (2021, November). *Spotlight on...performance- and image-enhancing drugs*. https://www.emcdda.europa.eu/spotlights/performance-and-image-enhancing-drugs_en

European Monitoring Centre for Drugs and Drug Addiction. (2022). *European drug report 2022: Trends and developments*. Publications Office of the European Union.

Ford, J. A., Pomykacz, C., Veliz, P., McCabe, S. E., & Boyd, C. J. (2018). Sports involvement, injury history, and non-medical use of prescription opioids among college students: An analysis with a national sample. *The American Journal on Addictions*, *27*(1), 15–22. https://doi.org/10.1111/ajad.12657

Gelber, J. (2021, June 29). How Len Bias's death helped launch the U.S.'s unjust war on drugs. *The Guardian*. https://www

.theguardian.com/sport/2021/jun/29/len-bias-death-basketball-war-on-drugs

Haffajee, R. L., & Mauri, A. (2021). Cannabis legalization in the U.S.: Population health impacts. *Health Affairs.* https://www.healthaffairs.org/do/10.1377/hpb20210701.500845/full/

Hasin, D., & Walsh, C. (2021). Trends over time in adult cannabis use: A review of recent findings. *Current Opinion in Psychology, 38,* 80–85. https://doi.org/10.1016/j.copsyc.2021.03.005

Henning, A., McLean, K., Andreasson, J., & Dimeo, P. (2021). Risk and enabling environments in sport: Systematic doping as harm reduction. *International Journal of Drug Policy, 91,* 102897. https://doi.org/10.1016/j.drugpo.2020.102897

Ingle, S. (2013, December 27). Memorable moments of 2013: Lance Armstrong admits that he doped. *The Guardian.* https://www.theguardian.com/sport/2013/dec/27/memorable-moments-2013-lance-armstrong

Kaplan, E. (2020, April 30). *How weed became "whatever": Leagues are ditching old policies.* ESPN.Com. https://www.espn.com/nfl/story/_/id/29114415/future-marijuana-drug-policy-nfl-pro-sports

Klosok, A. (n.d.). ROC at Beijing 2022: What is it and how can Russian athletes compete at the Olympics? *CNN.* https://www.cnn.com/2022/02/02/sport/roc-winter-olympics-beijing-russia-spt-intl/index.html

Kuhn, C., Foster, J., Wilson, L., Swartzwelder, S., & Wilson, W. (2019). *Buzzed: The straight facts about the most used and abused drugs from Alcohol to Ecstasy* (5th ed.). W. W. Norton.

Miller, K. E., Melnick, M. J., Farrell, M. P., Sabo, D. F., & Barnes, G. M. (2006). Jocks, gender, Binge drinking, and adolescent violence. *Journal of Interpersonal Violence, 21*(1), 105–120. https://doi.org/10.1177/0886260505281662

Munson, L. (2013, May 14). *Enforcer's family vs. the NHL.* ESPN. https://www.espn.com/espn/otl/story/_/id/9275330/looking-answers-derek-boogaard-death

n.a. (2014, January 28). *Survey reveals that majority of Americans believe Olympics less enjoyable due to doping*. Business Wire. https://www.businesswire.com/news/home/20140128005319/en/Survey-Reveals-That-Majority-of-Americans-Believe-Olympics-Less-Enjoyable-Due-to-Doping

Reinarman, C. (1994). The social construction of drug scares. In *Constructions of deviance: Social power, context, and interaction* (pp. 92–104). Wadsworth Publishing.

Rhodes, T. (2009). Risk environments and drug harms: A social science for harm reduction approach. *International Journal of Drug Policy*, *20*(3), 193–201. https://doi.org/10.1016/j.drugpo.2008.10.003

Ritchie, H., & Roser, M. (2018). *Opioids, cocaine, cannabis, and other illicit drugs*. Our World in Data. https://ourworldindata.org/illicit-drug-use

UK Anti-Doping. (n.d.). *Fast facts about steroids*. https://www.ukad.org.uk/fast-facts-about-steroids

U.S. Department of Health and Human Services, Substance Abuse and Mental Health Services Administration, Center for Behavioral Health Statistics and Quality. (2020). *National survey on drug use and health 2020*. Substance Abuse and Mental Health Services Administration. https://datafiles.samhsa.gov/

U.S. Drug Enforcement Adminstration. (2020). *Drug fact sheet: Kratom*. https://www.dea.gov/sites/default/files/2020-06/Kratom-2020_0.pdf

World Anti-Doping Agency. (2022). *2022 List of prohibited substances and methods*. https://www.wada-ama.org/en/resources/world-anti-doping-program/prohibited-list

Zinberg, N. (1986). *Drug, set, and setting: The basis for controlled intoxicant use*. Yale University Press.

CHAPTER 2

Epidemiology and History of Drug Use in Sport

Any discussion of the epidemiology of drug use in sport must confront a fundamental research dilemma: how do we know which and how many athletes use psychoactive substances? Moreover, how can we discern the specific substances that are consumed, with what frequency and in what quantity? These questions do not even broach the issue of motivation(s) for substance use, and their relationship to individuals' athletic endeavors. Nevertheless, such inquiries are necessary to recognizing the stark limitations of available data concerning psychoactive substance use in sport; indeed, they simultaneously illuminate the dubious quality of all data on population levels of drug consumption. The issues afflicting substance use statistics, within any group, may be simplified into two primary problems: one of scope, the other of accuracy. Even within more delimited participant pools, drug screening is not, and will never be, comprehensive. The most rigorously tested individuals—from elite athletes to those under criminal justice control—cannot be tested every day of their lives. Such a system would be tyrannical, inordinately expensive, and logistically impossible; as with any other oppressive regime, it might also encourage new methods of evading its totalitarian logic, an eventuality that points to the second problem with drugs data. Objective biometric tests are fallible, whether in the reliability of their chemical assays (contingent on a range of individual physiological factors) or in the fidelity of sample collection. Furthermore, appraising the accumulated research on population substance use, biological specimen analysis is the exception. The bulk of drug use data derives from self-report, or asking individuals themselves to confess their involvement in behaviors that may be stigmatized, contextually prohibited, or patently illegal. Even mundane forms of psychoactive substance use may be poorly represented within self-report surveys, vulnerable to recall bias, if not self-censorship (see, for example, Harrison, 1995; Khalili et al., 2021; Magura et al., 1999; Reuter et al., 2021).

If marred by the same flaws as all research on drugs, the blind spots characterizing athlete-specific data are relatively easy to map. Indeed, they will appear glaringly in the literature and statistical review that follow. The unique, if interrelated, issues of quality and scope arguably undermine the understanding of different athlete populations to different degrees. With few exceptions, drug use data drawing from biometric screens are limited to professional and elite amateur athletes (including those in high-level college sports). Thus, the "best" data neglects the vast majority of athletes—nonelites or amateurs, more generally—while further sketching but a partial profile of its subjects. Drug surveillance is invariably concentrated around or during periods of competition, with only the very top performers in each sport subjected to random testing in the "off-season." Any long-term fan will also intuit the gaps inherent in historical drug testing data in their favorite sport, as new substances, used for pleasure and/or performance, are constantly emerging—and being targeted by testing authorities. While elite athletes may sometimes be captured in self-report studies, the latter are more likely to represent lower-level or casual sports participants. Surveys utilizing self-report measures of substance use have the potential to be widely distributed, yet they are still relatively confined to certain demographic strata, namely school- and college-aged athletes. Such athletes are reachable by virtue of their affiliation with an educational and/or recreational institution—institutions whose membership terms may forbid drug use, a factor that disincentivizes truthfulness. Problems of social-desirability bias, or the tendency to underreport stigmatized behaviors, similarly stymie self-response studies of elite athletes, whose careers might further be compromised were anonymity breached (de Hon et al., 2015). Finally, while certain surveys may be administered longitudinally (e.g., the U.S. National College Health Assessment), data on any particular individual is likely to be cross-sectional, or reflective of one point in time. Moving on to both recent and historical prevalence statistics concerning psychoactive drug use in sport, we must keep in mind that this is a fractured landscape on shaky ground.

Current Prevalence Estimates for Psychoactive Substance Use Among Athletes

As the foregoing discussion began to lay out, it is difficult to make generalizable statements about the prevalence of psychoactive drug use among athletes, that is, the proportion of athletes who have recently, or ever, used substances that may alter their mood, awareness, thoughts, feelings, or behavior. Among other reasons, this is because athletes at different competition levels are required to submit to varying degrees, schedules, and types of drug screening—if they are mandated to test at all. In other words, it is not clear whether comparable data is available for both elite and nonelite athletes. Moreover, patterns of psychoactive substance use may be legitimately dependent on individuals' elite or professional status, which will certainly shape both the rewards and the consequences of drug consumption, as well as the likelihood of detection. Thus, we will consider the behaviors of these two groups separately, a division that also correlates with different source data: (largely) official reports of clinical drug testing for the former and scholarly or nongovernmental self-report surveys for the latter. While we will merely distinguish between the prevalence of psychoactive substance use among elite and nonelite athletes here, Chapter 3 will take up the "why" and the "how" of these disparities through the application of different theoretical lenses.

Drug Use at the Top: What Do We Know?

A wealth of drug screening data, current and historical, is available for athletes who represent the very best in their respective sports. However, we should not here mistake information quantity for quality, especially given our focus on psychoactive substances. First, mandatory drug screens for elite athletes are predictably geared toward the detection of doping drugs (as well as techniques and behaviors). For this reason, substances that are not defined as "performance enhancing" may not be targeted in testing; indeed, World Anti-Doping Agency (WADA) only reports three categories of psychoactive substances—stimulants, "narcotics," and cannabinoids—a list that neglects some of the most commonly used drugs, such as benzodiazepines, psychedelics, inhalants, alcohol, and nicotine. Second, elite athlete testing disproportionately occurs in the run-up to major competitions, when drug use that is not intended to improve performance may be abandoned. Third, while some statistics may be international in scope (such as those published by WADA, FIFA, or the

Association of Tennis Professionals/Women's Tennis Association [ATP/WTA]), the underlying data often derives from national sports or antidoping organizations, whose testing efforts may be uneven. Finally, at the time of writing, the most recent data from the many antidoping institutions drew on tests from 2020, a year in which both screening schedules and athlete substance use may have veered from baseline levels, as major sporting events were canceled or deferred, and National Anti-Doping Agencies (NADOs) reduced their activities to "mission critical" levels (U.S. Anti-Doping Agency [USADA], 2020).

Perhaps the widest ranging repository of information on elite athletes' substance use, the WADA collates international testing results from its national-level member organizations (NADOs), producing annual publications that include top-level amateur, professional, and Paralympic athletes. If limited in its reporting of psychoactive drugs to those enumerated on its "Banned Substances List," the sheer bulk of WADA test data does allow us to begin making out the demographic contours of drug use in this rarefied population—patterns that may resonate with those among less accomplished athletes. The yearly *Anti-Doping Testing Figures Report* reports adverse (AAF) and atypical test findings (ATF)—drug "positive" results—by gender, sport, organization, and substance. Although the underlying analytic unit is a drug test (not an individual athlete), these reports nevertheless permit the calculation of basic prevalence statistics for the three categories of psychoactive substance mentioned previously. Still, without knowing the proportion of athletes tested by sport, country, or competition, these figures must be interpreted cautiously, especially since they obscure the national test protocols that feed them. In 2020, WADA reported the analysis of 149,758 "samples," of which 1,009 were associated with AAFs—a tentative positive rate of 0.67% across all substances. (For reference, 2019 testing data showed a AAF percentage of 0.97%, suggesting that 2020 findings may be atypical.) Even as a prevalence below 1% would reveal elite athletes to be strongly protected against psychoactive substance use, further investigation diminishes this percentage dramatically; the vast majority of AAFs in WADA data reflect the detection of performance-enhancing substances or techniques without psychoactive properties. Among 1,503 AAF "occurrences," only 225 involved stimulants (e.g., methylphenidate or Ritalin, cocaine), 42 detected cannabinoids (diverse psychoactive compounds found within cannabis), and 4 found narcotics (e.g., oxycodone, morphine) (World Anti-Doping Agency, 2020). Drug-specific prevalence rates cannot be calculated, given that multiple substances within each category may be identified within a single sample; instead, we present the proportion of all adverse analytic findings that contained psychoactive substances in Table 1.

Table 1: Adverse Analytic Findings by Substance Type

	Number AAF Occurrences	% AAF Occurrences
All Substances	1,503	100
All Psychoactive Substances	271	18.03
Stimulants	225	15.00
Cannabinoids	42	2.80
Narcotics	4	0.27

Source: WADA, 2020

WADA's 2020 *Anti-Doping Figures* also provide some information on banned substance, and psychoactive substance, use by type of sport, gender, and season; again, however, without knowledge of the denominator within each sport, the first two prevalence figures must be acknowledged as artifacts of testing procedures. Looking at sports by their inclusion in Olympic competition, analyses reveal a significantly higher proportion of AAFs among samples from non-Olympic athletes. Where 0.48% of Olympic sport samples suggested the use of banned substances or techniques, 1.78% of non-Olympic sport samples were flagged for adverse analytic findings. Interestingly, AAFs specific to each class of psychoactive substance highlighted a unique set of sports. Samples taken from athletes competing in track and field ("Athletics"), powerlifting, "aquatics" (e.g., swimming, diving, water polo), football, and weightlifting showed the most positives for stimulants, while basketball was the only sport associated with more than two cannabinoid AAFs. With regard to "narcotics," four sports each reported one positive sample: volleyball, American football, canoeing/kayaking, and ultratriathalon. Adverse analytic findings (for all banned drugs and techniques) by gender showed near parity between male and female athletes, at 0.7% and 0.6% of samples, respectively. Finally, the likelihood of an AAF appears highly elevated when a sample is drawn "in competition," with 1.2% of such samples flagged, compared to only 0.34% of those collected out of "competition."

Looking at one international member federation whose antidoping efforts contribute to WADA's annual reports can give us a sense of their infinitesimal scope. The International Football Federation, or FIFA, comprises 211 member associations, who in turn represent not only the same number of national teams, but nearly 4,000 professional clubs, and an excess of 128,000 career players (International Football Federation, n.d.). Yet in its 2020–2021 *Anti-Doping Report*, FIFA describes annual testing results for 354 players, or roughly 0.28% of professional world footballers. Relying on a "shared responsibility" with both member associations and the regional confederations to perform antidoping tests, FIFA limits its own direct testing involvement to FIFA-sponsored and Olympic competitions, registering a presence at five total events from July 2020 to June 2021. Among the 602 samples solicited by FIFA over this 12-month period, at least 1 player from 50 national teams and 2 players from 6 club teams were represented; none were flagged for adverse findings, suggesting a prevalence of 0% for banned stimulant, narcotic, and cannabis usage among professional footballers—or at least among the quarter-of-a-percent selected (International Football Federation, 2021).

In highlighting the extremely limited reach of antidoping tests, the intention is not to advocate for more extensive or stringent antidoping endeavors; rather, this context must necessarily constrain our interpretation of the data. It is possible, of course, that this testing data is an undistorted window into elite athlete substance use. In 2021, U.S. Major League Baseball conducted 8,436 drug tests among only 1,200 players—in theory, 7 temporally distinct tests per player, both in- and off-season. Nevertheless, only six tests were declared positive for any banned substance and but one for a psychoactive (stimulant) (Martin, 2021). Similarly, all participants in international professional tennis events are subjected to antidoping controls each year, with individual players typically tested multiple times. In 2021, only one of nearly 5,000 samples detected a prohibited psychoactive substance (again, a stimulant) (International Tennis Federation [ITF], 2021). Corroborating both trends, albeit within a vastly different sport, the mixed martial arts Ultimate Fighting Championship (UFC) performed over 4,000 tests of 749 athletes in 2021, but sanctioned only two that year—for modafinil and cocaine, both controlled stimulants (UFC Anti-Doping Program, 2021).

If largely confirming elite athletes' low rates of psychoactive drug use relative to the general population, studies relying on self-disclosure nevertheless betray higher levels than suggested by blood and urine screens, while also providing a sharper focus on certain kinds of substance use within specific sporting populations (de Hon et al., 2015; Exner et al., 2021). In fact, a 2015 review showed that doping control test results typically estimated banned substance use at 1% to 2%, while questionnaire studies of elite athletes yielded estimates ranging from 1% to 70% (de Hon et al., 2015). Importantly, such research estimates the consumption of substances that are not monitored by antidoping authorities, including alcohol and nicotine—that is, the drugs most used by elite (and nonelite) athletes. Among the former population, alcohol use and overuse, in the forms of binge and heavy drinking, may be more prevalent within team and contact sports, with some outliers. Surveys undertaken among "Division 1" (D1) college athletes in the United States show that nearly three-quarters consumed alcohol in the previous year, with 44% "typically" imbibing four or more drinks per drinking occasion (National Collegiate Athletic Association [NCAA], 2018). Among men, the highest rates of alcohol consumption were observed among elite participants in ice hockey (92%), lacrosse (88%), and swimming (88%)—results that nearly mirror those among female athletes, where field hockey (94%), lacrosse (92%), and swimming (92%) topped the table. Such findings resonate with those from professional sports leagues; a 2014–2015 survey of alcohol use in Australasia's National Rugby League Premiership revealed "hazardous levels" among 68.6% of players in the preseason, and 62.8% during the competition period, levels that in fact exceed those in the general population (Du Preez et al., 2017). Moving to the second most prevalent substance in its most commonly used form, cigarettes (and all inhaled forms of nicotine, including vapes) are consumed far less frequently by elite athletes, perhaps for obvious reasons related to performance. Only 9.2% of D1 student-athletes said that they had smoked a cigarette in the previous year, although "spit tobacco" use was more popular, at 13% overall. Moreover, nearly half of male baseball (46%) and ice hockey (44%) players reported consuming the product, a habit that many may sustain into their professional careers. Studies of American Major League Baseball players have repeatedly shown over one-third of players to "chew" (smokeless tobacco) (Conrad et al., 2015; Severson et al., 2005)

Where anecdotal evidence suggests that cannabis consumption is common, if not normalized, within some professional sports, scholarly research cannot yet confirm. Cannabis is certainly the most prevalent illicit substance within elite college sports samples in the United States—nearly 18% of Division 1 athletes reported past-year cannabis use in 2017, while 0.5% reported ingestion of synthetic cannabinoids (NCAA, 2018). Such figures may be peculiar to this age group and geographic setting. While limited, other studies have found significantly lower levels of recent cannabis consumption among elite athletes, with estimates ranging from 3% to 10% (Brisola-Santos et al., 2016; Diehl et al., 2014; Dunn, 2011; Thevis, 2008). Figures concerning past-year cocaine use within this population are more on par with other national samples: 2.6% among U.S. Division I athletes and 3.2% among a group of elite Australian athletes (Dunn, 2011; NCAA, 2018). Finally, data on other forms of illicit drug use are even more rare, circumscribed, and dated. The same survey of eight Australian national sport organizations found modest rates of recent ecstasy (MDMA) (3.7%), methamphetamine (1%), GHB (0.4%), and ketamine use (0.2%) (Dunn, 2011). And while the NCAA's (2018) recurring survey seeks to capture the use of ecstasy, "narcotic" painkillers, and attention-deficit/hyperactivity disorder (ADHD) stimulant medications (without a prescription), results are not disaggregated by division. Nevertheless, levels of such drug consumption among all student-athletes are significantly lower than those reported by 18- to 25-year-old's in the general population (U.S. Department of Health and Human Services, Substance Abuse and Mental Health Services Administration, Center for Behavioral Health Statistics and Quality, 2018). Across all categories of illicit drug use documented in self-disclosure surveys of elite athletes, males appear to be more likely consumers, whether in university, national, or professional competition. Moreover, certain sports are repeatedly represented with the higher echelons of licit and illicit drug use, as measured by both biometric screens and self-report studies, namely, lacrosse, swimming/aquatics, ice hockey, field hockey, golf, field hockey, rugby, track/athletics, and volleyball. Both of these demographic and team trends hold among nonelites, where significantly larger study samples have been surveyed.

Psychoactive Drug Use Among Nonelite and Everyday Athletes

Given the literature reviewed previously, it will perhaps be unsurprising that much of the research on nonelite athletes' use of psychoactive substance also derives from university- or school-aged athletes in the United States, with some sport- and drug-specific exceptions gathered across the globe. Notably, there exists a wealth of studies on the use of (and connections between) image and performance enhancing drug (IPED) and psychoactive substance use among gymgoers, while researchers have responded to recent trends in opioid and cannabis use by reviewing the extent of data that is specific to athletes. Nevertheless, the large, public-facing datasets that are summarized are largely confined to U.S. academic contexts. Several explanations may be proffered for these particular geographic and demographic biases: the convenience of capturing research participants within institutional contexts, an overwhelming interest in describing—and reducing—potentially harmful behaviors among adolescents and young adults, and the long-standing cultural and political fixation on psychoactive drug use in the United States. The unique imbrication of university and professional athletics in the United States, where institutions of secondary and higher education often serve as "feeders" to the major leagues and Olympic teams, may also explain the concentration of research among student-athletes. Some research among elite athletes, employing both drug tests and individual interviews, has revealed the tendency of some athletes to underreport their own substance use, a limitation that should be kept in mind in reviewing the data in this section, all of which derives from self-disclosure studies (USADA, 2020).

Studies of elite populations seem to indicate that the prevalence of psychoactive substance use is inverse to the level of competition, with antidoping tests performed under the auspices of WADA and professional leagues yielding adverse findings in less than 1% of cases. While the cogency of this conclusion cannot be assured in light of patchy data from disparate sources, a comparative assessment of drug use across different divisions of college athletics appears to validate it. Returning to the NCAA's quadrennial survey of more than 20,000 student-athletes, nearly every form of substance use showed consistent increases from Division I to Division III athletes (where disaggregated data was available), as summarized in Table 2; past-year consumption of the two most common illicit drugs, marijuana and cocaine, doubled or nearly doubled from the top to the lowest division.

Table 2: Self-reported Past-Year Substance Use Among Divisions I, II, and III Athletes

Substance Type	Division I	Division II	Division III
Alcohol	74.5	74	81.1
Cigarettes	9.2	9.6	12.2
Spit Tobacco	12.7	13.5	14
Cocaine	2.6	2.9	5.3
Marijuana	17.7	21.6	32.6
Synthetic Marijuana	0.5	0.9	0.8

Source: NCAA, 2018

A range of scholarly studies considering different athlete populations across the world have validated this disjuncture between elite and nonelite athlete consumption of psychoactive substances. Looking at the psychoactive drug most widely used in sport—cannabis—research investigating football players in Cameroon, adolescents in France, and teenage German athletes uniformly revealed higher levels of consumption among self-identified "amateurs," "informal" sports participants, and nonelite athletes (Ama et al., 2003; Brisola-Santos et al., 2016; Diehl et al., 2014; Lentillon-Kaestner & Ohl, 2011; Peretti-Watel & Lorente, 2004). While the next chapter will lay out theoretical explanations for such disparities, it may be relevant here to note the seasonality of athlete substance use, as captured by the NCAA, as this phenomenon may reflect similar considerations on the part of individual athletes. Asked whether they had used each drug "only during the competitive season," "only during the off-season," or "during both the competitive and off-seasons," athletes disproportionately selected the second time frame, for every psychoactive substance with the exception of alcohol. Suggesting that many, if not most, athletes view drug use as a possible impediment to their performance level, we might tentatively conclude that more elite competitors also perceive a greater disincentive to consumption.

The estimates presented in Table 2 may leave some to wonder whether less elite athletics participation may in fact represent a risk factor for substance use, with over 80% of D3 athletes recently consuming alcohol and almost one-third reporting marijuana use; indeed, outside of elite circles, sports involvement shows an inconsistent relationship with substance use, varying by both specific sport, sex, and substance. On the one hand, both U.S. national data on age-graded drug use and comparative studies within college populations reveal sports participation to be unrelated to or protective against most illicit drug and nicotine use; in other words, nonathletes tend to smoke, sniff, and otherwise consume psychoactive drugs at levels that are similar to or higher than their athlete peers (with some exceptions.). For example, the 2018 U.S. National Survey on Drug Use and Health found that 34.8% and 5.8% of all young adults aged 18 to 25 had used marijuana and cocaine, respectively, in the past year, rates that are slightly higher than those captured by the NCAA. Studies focusing specifically on illicit substance use behaviors among college-enrolled athletes and nonathletes have found similar, though sometimes nonsignificant differences (Dunn & Wang, 2003; Lane & DeCamp, 2017; Lisha & Sussman, 2010; Pate et al., 2000; Yusko et al., 2008). Through a secondary analysis of the U.S. College Risk Behavior Survey, Lane and Decamp (2017) demonstrated that college athletes were less likely to smoke cigarettes and marijuana and use "other drugs" than their peers outside athletics—but by slim margins. Similarly, Lisha and Sussman's (2010) systematic review of research on the effect of college sports participation on illicit drug use found that the bulk of studies (60%) showed an inverse relationship between athletic involvement and marijuana and "other drug" consumption; two additional projects concluded that there was no relationship between athletic status and illicit drug use, while the remaining articles delineated an elevated risk only within certain athlete or "exerciser" subpopulations—a finding that will be explored further later on (Anderson, 1991; Dunn & Wang, 2003). In an analysis of college students, Ford (2007) identified male ice hockey and female soccer players as reporting significantly higher rates of marijuana use than nonathletes, although, across the board, male athletes consumed illicit drugs at lower levels than their peers outside of sports, and no differences were found among females on the basis of athletic participation. Ultimately, only one study of illegal substance use among school-age athletes has identified sports involvement as an overarching risk factor for initiation, but with gender-specific effects; focusing on high school athletes, Ewing (1998) showed that males competing across all sports consumed marijuana at elevated levels. Even while relatively recent reviews have shown an increasing level of cannabis consumption, in particular, among athletes worldwide (23.4%), this figure still remains significantly below that of nonathletes (Docter et al., 2020).

Of course, the category of psychoactive substances spans the border of legality, which is itself characterized by gray areas. Where a wealth of research has shown a positive relationship between alcohol consumption and participation in (nonelite) college athletics, a handful of studies additionally suggest that certain subsamples may engage in the nonmedical use of prescription opioid (NUPO) painkillers (e.g., oxycodone, hydrocodone) as a consequence of their sports involvement. Lane and Decamp (2017) found that college athletes reported past-year drinking and binge drinking at significantly higher levels than their nonathlete counterparts, a conclusion reiterated by more than 75% of studies analyzed by the same systematic review cited previously (Lisha & Sussman, 2010). Research outside the U.S. has also suggested that sports participation may contribute to alcohol initiation and drinking levels over time; in a longitudinal study of Norwegian adolescents, Wichstrøm and Wichstrøm (2009) demonstrated that individuals confirming sports involvement in the first wave of data collection reported more frequent episodes of alcohol intoxication at subsequent time points. (Given the strength of the research association between alcohol and athletics, Chapter 4 will consider specific sports risk environments for drinking in depth.) Interestingly, one study showed that sex moderated the relationship between sports involvement and alcohol consumption, with female athletes more likely to drink than their nonathlete student peers (Pate et al., 2000). Finally, recent contributions to the literature have isolated athletic participation as a risk factor for NUPO among certain high school and college athletes. Drawing on survey data encompassing over 300,000 college student-athletes, Ford et al. (2018) determined that varsity athletes were about 26% more likely to engage in NUPO than students who did not participate in competitive sports; male athletes, injured athletes, and injured male athletes indicated significantly higher levels of nonmedical prescription opioid use, with nearly 18% of the last group reporting consumption in the past year alone. Although failing to find a blanket association between sports and NUPO, Veliz et al. (2013, 2014) did highlight specific subgroups at risk, namely, male athletes, as well as (American) football and wrestling participants. While the use of potent analgesic-type drugs may be intuitive among individuals prone to injury or even training-related soreness, Chapter 5 will consider the ways in which specific sports and policy contexts promote prescription and other opioid use outside of medical supervision.

One population that diverges from the substance use trends outlined previously are gymgoers, who may participate in competitive bodybuilding or weightlifting but are more defined by their involvement in training than in organized competition. Unlike many of the studies reviewed previously, research on gymgoers is less centered within the United States and further captures a wider age range; it has also suggested that such "recreational" fitness populations may represent the majority of IPED consumers—not professional athletes (Salinas et al., 2019). Moreover, multiple studies have captured relatively high levels of psychoactive substance use within such fitness populations, a phenomenon that may be connected to their consumption of anabolic–androgenic steroids (AAS). For example, a 2017 national survey of individuals who use IPED in the United Kingdom found that 33% had used cannabis in the past year, 25% cocaine, 14% MDMA, and nearly 7% amphetamine—levels in excess of not only other athletes, but the general population (Begley et al., 2017; Broadfield, 2017; U.S. Department of Health and Human Services, Substance Abuse and Mental Health Services Administration, Center for Behavioral Health Statistics and Quality, 2016). Similar results have been found among gym users, weightlifters, and bodybuilders in diverse countries, including the United States, Ireland, Sweden, France, Norway, Australia, and Iran (Abrahin et al., 2017; Havnes et al., 2021; Jennings et al., 2014; Kanayama et al., 2003; McVeigh et al., 2021; Sagoe et al., 2015; Skarberg et al., 2009; Turnock, 2021; Van de Ven et al., 2018). As these studies show, motivations for concurrent IPED and psychoactive drugs use are myriad, with some psychoactive substances used to support training or weight loss, while others ameliorate the side effects associated with AAS, in particular (Jennings et al., 2014; Sagoe et al., 2015; Zahnow et al., 2018). Some scholars have additionally explored the use of IPED as embedded within gym and bodybuilding cultures, a thread that will be explored more fully in the next chapter, where the sequential link between IPED and other substances will also be considered (van de Ven & Mulrooney, 2017).

Is This Normal? Historical Trends in Psychoactive Substance Use Among Athletes

A cursory review of major news headlines in the run-up to any major sports competition might lead one to conclude that substance use—whether psychoactive, performance enhancing, or somewhere in between—is epidemic and rising among athletes. However, such a conclusion is hardly supported by the available data, which is, at best, uneven and discontinuous. It is interesting to consider why a subject surrounded by so much social concern and moral fervor is so poorly documented historically. Arguably, the paucity of systematic data on athletes' substance use is a rational outcome of the system designed to address this behavior: antidoping policy and ideology. While couching their actions in the language of not only fairness, but individual health, antidoping institutions punish athletes found to have ingested banned substances, a practice that has the logical effect of making many kinds of substance use clandestine in this population. The antidoping movement solidified in the late 1950s and early 1960s, informed by a growing body of research on performance-enhancing drug use among elite athletes; ironically, the draconian policies that were crafted to address this "problem" cut short attempts to properly characterize it, leaving researchers with little comparable data over the past half-century.

Interestingly, the specific (category of) substances that mobilized "moral entrepreneurship" against doping were well-known stimulants, used within the general population for their psychoactive effects: amphetamines (Becker, 1997; Dimeo, 2007). While consumed in a variety of preparations (e.g., amphetamine sulfate, methamphetamine), the use of amphetamines in elite-level sports competitions spread in the aftermath of World War II, becoming the "most commonly used drug in sports" between 1948 and the early 1970s (Dimeo, 2007, p. 67; Donohoe & Johnson, 1986). If hardly systematic, research from this era suggests significant use of amphetamines within cycling, professional football (American and European), and track—endurance sports that benefitted from a long-acting stimulant. Before the official prohibition of amphetamines in cycling in 1966, testing among Belgian riders revealed a prevalence of 37% among professionals and 23% among amateurs; similarly, screenings of Italian football players in 1967 showed 36% to be positive for amphetamines (Council of Europe, 1964, cited in Dimeo, 2007). Anecdotal evidence from American football, published in media reports, interviews, and personal memoirs, intimate that amphetamine consumption among players was not only widespread but also effectively institutionalized, with team trainers and physicians distributing the drugs to players in large quantities (Dimeo, 2007). With the implementation of amphetamine (and other doping) bans, reliable testing, and related sanctions in the mid-1960s, evidence of amphetamine and other psychoactive drug use among elite athletes declined, although we cannot conclude that consumption simply ceased. (Indeed, the 2012 revelation of the "most sophisticated, professionalized and successful doping program the sport [cycling] has ever seen" betrays the ways in which prohibition has altered, though not eliminated, drug use in that sport, among others, Fotheringham, 2012).

Apart from explaining the legal origins of our current blind spots concerning drug use in sport, the example of methamphetamine illustrates another trend in athletes' substance use, namely, its close correlation with consumption dynamics in the larger, nonathlete population. A potent weapon to combat solider fatigue during WWII, amphetamine was deployed among civilians in medical and quasi-medical ways in the years following the end of the war, while later finding a niche audience within youth and criminal subcultures. Pharmaceutical preparations such as Methedrine, Desoxyn, and Benzedrine were widely prescribed as "pep pills" and in vitamin-infused shots that countered physical and mental exhaustion, suppressed appetite, and imbued users with a general sense of well-being, if not euphoria. By 1962, 80,000 kg of amphetamine salts were produced in the United States—the equivalent of 43 doses for every individual in the country; contemporaneous dispensing data from the UK suggests that the level of amphetamine prescription might have consistently supplied 1% of the adult population with a daily dose (Rasmussen, 2008). While this history may seem esoteric, it also permits the contextual interpretation of more recent shifts in psychoactive drug use in sports: as goes the public, so go its athletes (at least, to a degree.) Although certain aspects of the sports risk (and protective) environments might account for unique levels of substance use among particular athletes, this fundamental recognition allows us to evaluate changes in the use of licit and illicit drugs in this population as "normal" or at least expected.

Unfortunately, the best longitudinal statistics on athletes' psychoactive substance use derive from a source fairly circumscribed in its scope: the NCAA's National Study on Substance Use Habits of College Student-Athletes in the United States, a quadrennial survey that has collected data since 1985. If limited to young adult athletes in but one country, the NCAA study does allow us to map substance use trends across several generations ("Gen X," "Millennials," and "Gen Z"), particularly for drugs with enduring popularity: marijuana, cocaine, alcohol, and nicotine. It is perhaps contrary to expectation that a multidecade review of NCAA survey results generally reveals falling rates of substance use across nearly every category (albeit with some nuance.) As shown in Table 3, college athletes' recent consumption of smokeless tobacco, alcohol, and marijuana declined between 1985 and 2017, although different peaks and valleys are observable throughout the years. Cocaine represents the singular exception to this rule over the full, nearly 40-year period, with systematic increases observed over each decade. It is here that we might look to the bigger picture of societal drug use to gain a helpful perspective. Since its inception in 1971, the National Survey on Drug Use and Health has observed nearly continuous decreases among young adults in their consumption of alcohol, all tobacco products, and even marijuana—although the most current data reveals an uptick in the use of that drug alongside local legalization statutes (also suggested by the NCAA survey.) Here too, cocaine has appeared as an outlier, with young adult prevalence rising almost 50% between 2011 and 2017 (U.S. Department of Health and Human Services, Substance Abuse and Mental Health Services Administration, Center for Behavioral Health Statistics and Quality, 2020).

Table 3: Self-reported Past-Year Substance Use Among NCAA Student-Athletes, 1985–2017

	1985	1989	1997	2009	2017
Alcohol	88	89	80.5	83	77
Marijuana	36	28	28.4	22.6	24.7
Smokeless Tobacco	20	28	22.5	17.4	13.4
Cocaine	17	5	1.5	1.8	3.8

Sources: NCAA, 2018; Green et al., 2001; Anderson, 1991

Certain latent trends in college athletes' psychoactive drug use are not captured in Table 3, as continuous data is not available; this may point to both a strength and a weakness of the NCAA instrument, which is constantly updated to capture novel (and remove passé) substances. For example, measures of nonmedical "narcotic painkiller" use were added to the survey in 2009, with a decade's worth of research showing a significant drop in athletes' consumption of painkillers without a prescription. The 2017 survey included the first item concerning past-year "e-cigarette" use, and while historical evidence is thus outstanding, levels of vaping by academic standing may provide some hints; in 2017, the highest prevalence of e-cigarette use was reported by freshmen athletes.

Having started this chapter with a review of current drug testing data from the WADA, it may make sense to return for historical statistics, fully cognizant of their limitations. In fact, archived information on "adverse analytical findings" or AAFs detected by WADA labs goes back to only 2013, while results disaggregated by substance are not presented before the most recent report. Of course, WADA itself is just over 20 years old and was created to promote and enforce a standardized antidoping code across international sport. Thus, the data presented in Table 4 is international in scope but limited to a single generation of the world's most elite athletes. It should be noted that so-called AAFs, while highlighting the presence of a banned substance in an individual's blood or urine, do not necessary translate into antidoping rule violations, or ADRVs; a significant number may be ruled "therapeutic use exemptions," for which athletes have received special medical approval, or even erroneous findings. The following numbers are almost certainly dominated by (suspected) performance-enhancing substances or by-products, without psychoactive effects, a fundamental outcome of testing protocols that are framed in terms of "fair competition," with athlete health (arguably) a secondary consideration.

Table 4: Adverse Analytical Findings from WADA Testing, 2013-2019

	2013	2014	2015	2016	2017	2018	2019
#AAFs	2,540	2,287	2,522	3,032	2,749	2,771	2,701
%AAFs*	1.2	1.1	1.1	1.3	1.1	1.1	1.0
% Male	80	79	79	79	78	77	77
% IC**	78	78	76	78	81	77	75

Source: World Anti-Doping Agency (2013, 2014, 2015, 2016, 2017, 2018, 2019)

* = % of all testing samples showing AAFs
** = in-competition

Keeping these caveats in mind, it seems nevertheless clear that elite athletes' consumption of banned substances has been relatively stable over the past decade, if not trending downward. Since 2013, 1% to 1.3% of samples have been flagged as "atypical" or "adverse," with the vast majority collected from male athletes during competition periods (IC). Given the latter fact, it is unsurprising that AAFs locally peaked in 2016, the only Summer Olympics year included in the table. (Roughly four times as many athletes compete in the summer, compared to the winter, Olympics. Finally, these results confirm the gendered dynamics of drug use in sport found throughout the literature, which consistently show male athletes to be at greater risk. Still, we should not walk away from this data before once more grasping its weaknesses. Not only does biological testing yield findings only for a select number of prohibited drugs, but the testing regime itself suppresses the behavior of interest. Where trend data may be more solid than estimates of absolute substance use prevalence, it will still fail to capture emerging substances, the development and use of which is incentivized by the current "banned list."

Reflection Points

1. How does psychoactive substance use in sport reflect, or anticipate, broader substance use trends in the general population?

2. How might we collect better data on psychoactive substance use among athletes, at all levels of competition?

3. How should we evaluate sports-specific substance use policies? How effective are psychoactive substance use prohibitions, compared to those affecting society at large?

4. How might the reliability of self-disclosure, or drug testing data, be affected by shifting morality around cannabis or nicotine products?

Glossary

Antidoping: An ideology and practice that prohibits certain substances, or practices, among elite athletes, for self-stated reasons of fairness, athlete health, and the "spirit of sport"

Elite or High-Performance Sport: The highest level of competition within a particular sport or athlete population. Examples of elite sport include professional leagues, national teams, and Division I college competition.

Epidemiology: The study of the distribution and determinants of health-related conditions and behaviors within specific populations

Prevalence: A measure of frequency within a specified group; used with epidemiology, prevalence commonly refers to the proportion of a population that engages in a certain health-related behaviors or that is experiencing a particular health condition.

Prohibited or Banned Substances: Substances that athletes, participating in certain competitions, teams, or leagues, cannot ingest without special permission, due to their suspected enhancement of athletic performance

Recall Bias: Error that is present within self-report studies, as a consequence of participants' inability to accurately remember certain events, beyond a particular time frame; recall bias may be nonrandom or unequally distributed across different participant groups.

Stigma: A negative label or understanding of a trait, behavior, or group as undesirable, abnormal, or deviant

REFERENCES

Abrahin, O., Félix Souza, N. S., de Sousa, E. C., Santos, A. M., & Bahrke, M. S. (2017). Anabolic–androgenic steroid use among Brazilian women: An exploratory investigation. *Journal of Substance Use*, *22*(3), 246–252. https://doi.org/10.1080/1465 9891.2016.1179806

Ama, P. F. M., Betnga, B., Ama Moor, V. J., & Kamga, J. P. (2003). Football and doping: Study of African amateur footballers. *British Journal of Sports Medicine*, *37*(4), 307–310. https://doi.org/10.1136/bjsm.37.4.307

Anderson, W. (1991). A national survey of alcohol and drug use by college athletes. *The Physician and Sportsmedicine*, *19*(2), 91–104. https://www.tandfonline.com/doi/abs/10.1080/0091384 7.1991.11702148

Becker, H. S. (1997). *Outsiders: Studies in sociology of deviance*. Free.

Begley, E., McVeigh, J., & Hope, V. (2017). *2016 National IPED info survey report*. Liverpool John Moores University. https://www.ipedinfo.co.uk/resources/downloads/2016%20 National%20IPED%20Info%20Survey%20report%20FINAL. pdf

Brisola-Santos, M. B., Gallinaro, J. G. de M. e, Gil, F., Sampaio-Junior, B., Marin, M. C. D., de Andrade, A. G., Richter, K. P., Glick, I. D., Baltieri, D. A., & Castaldelli-Maia, J. M. (2016). Prevalence and correlates of cannabis use among athletes—A systematic review. *The American Journal on Addictions*, *25*(7), 518–528. https://doi.org/10.1111/ajad.12425

Broadfield, D. (2017). *Drug misuse: Findings from the 2016/17 crime survey for England and Wales*. (p. 44). Statistical Bulletins—Home Office Statistics under the National Statistics Code of Practice.

Conrad, A. K., Hutton, S. B., Munnelly, M., & Bay, R. C. (2015). Screening for smokeless tobacco use and presence of oral lesions in major league baseball athletes. *Journal of the California Dental Association*, *43*(1), 14–20. https://doi.org/10 .1080/19424396.2015.12222801

de Hon, O., Kuipers, H., & van Bottenburg, M. (2015). Prevalence of doping use in elite sports: A review of numbers and methods. *Sports Medicine*, *45*(1), 57–69. https://doi.org/10.1007/s40279-014-0247-x

Diehl, K., Thiel, A., Zipfel, S., Mayer, J., & Schneider, S. (2014). Substance use among elite adolescent athletes: Findings from the GOAL Study. *Scandinavian Journal of Medicine & Science in Sports*, *24*(1), 250–258. https://doi.org/10.1111/j.1600-0838.2012.01472.x

Dimeo, P. (2007). *A history of drug use in sport 1876–1976: Beyond good and evil*. Routledge.

Docter, S., Khan, M., Gohal, C., Ravi, B., Bhandari, M., Gandhi, R., & Leroux, T. (2020). Cannabis use and sport: A systematic review. *Sports Health*, *12*(2), 189–199. https://doi.org/10.1177/1941738120901670

Donohoe, T., & Johnson, N. (1986). *Foul play: Drug abuse in sports*. B. Blackwell.

Dunn, M. (2011). Recreational substance use among Elite Australian athletes. *Drug and Alcohol Review*, *30*(1), 63–68. https://doi.org/10.1111/j.1465-3362.2010.00200.x

Dunn, M. S., & Wang, M. Q. (2003). Effects of physical activity on substance use among college students. *American Journal of Health Studies*, *18*(2/3), 126–132.

Du Preez, E. J., Graham, K. S., Gan, T. Y., Moses, B., Ball, C., & Kuah, D. E. (2017). Depression, anxiety, and alcohol use in elite rugby league players over a competitive season. *Clinical Journal of Sport Medicine*, *27*(6), 530–535. https://doi.org/10.1097/JSM.0000000000000411

Exner, J., Bitar, R., Berg, X., Pichler, E.-M., Herdener, M., Seifritz, E., & Claussen, M. C. (2021). Use of psychotropic substances among elite athletes—A narrative review. *Swiss Medical Weekly*, *151*, w20412. https://doi.org/10.4414/smw.2021.20412

Ewing, C. P. (1998). Introduction to Law Enforcement. *Behavioral Sciences & the Law, 16*(4), 391–392. a9h.

Ford, J. A. (2007). Substance Use Among College Athletes: A Comparison Based on Sport/Team Affiliation. *Journal of American College Health,* *55*(6), 367–373. https://doi.org/10.3200/JACH.55.6.367-373

Ford, J. A., Pomykacz, C., Veliz, P., McCabe, S. E., & Boyd, C. J. (2018). Sports involvement, injury history, and non-medical use of prescription opioids among college students: An analysis with a national sample: Sports and Non-Wedical Use of Prescription Opioids. *The American Journal on Addictions, 27*(1), 15–22. https://doi.org/10.1111/ajad.12657

Fotheringham, W. (2012, October 11). Lance Armstrong's team "ran most sophisticated doping programme ever." *The Guardian.* https://www.theguardian.com/sport/2012/oct/11/armstrong-usada-sophisticated-doping-scheme

Green, G. A., Uryasz, F. D., Petr, T. A., & Bray, C. D. (2001). NCAA Study of Substance Use and Abuse Habits of College Student-Athletes. *Clinical Journal of Sport Medicine, 11*(1), 51–56.

Harrison, L. (1995). The validity of self-reported data on drug use. *Journal of Drug Issues, 25*(1), 91–111.

Havnes, I. A., Jørstad, M. L., & Bjørnebekk, A. (2021). Double trouble? A mixed methods study exploring experiences with combined use of anabolic-androgenic steroids and psychoactive substances among women. *Performance Enhancement & Health, 9*(3), 100198. https://doi.org/10.1016/j.peh.2021.100198

International Football Federation. (2021). *Anti-doping report 2020–2021*. https://digitalhub.fifa.com/m/7ad5e7cef54f9000/original/FIFA-Anti-Doping-Report-2021-2022-ver2-indd.pdf

International Football Federation. (n.d.). *About FIFA: Member associations*. https://www.fifa.com/about-fifa/associations

International Olympic Committee. (2021a, December 14). *Tokyo 2020 facts and figures*. https://olympics.com/ioc/tokyo-2020-facts-and-figures

International Olympic Committee. (2021b). *Factsheet: The Olympic winter games* (p. 11). https://stillmed.olympics.com

/media/Documents/Olympic-Games/Factsheets/The-Olympic-Winter-Games.pdf#_ga=2.95447772.1387851327.1545035637-2118090758.1543323217

International Tennis Federation. (2021). *Tennis anti-doping programme quarterly report, July to September 2021*. https://antidoping.itftennis.com/antidoping/news/articles.aspx

Jennings, C., Patten, E., Kennedy, M., & Patten, C. (2014). *Examining the profile and perspectives of individuals attending harm reduction services who are users of performance and image enhancing drugs*. Merchants Quay Ireland, Homeless & Drug Services.

Kanayama, G., Cohane, G. H., & Pope, H. G. (2003). Past anabolic-androgenic steroid use among men admitted for substance abuse treatment: An underrecognized problem? *The Journal of Clinical Psychiatry*, *64*(2), 13902. https://doi.org/10.4088/jcp.v64n0208

Khalili, P., Nadimi, A. E., Baradaran, H. R., Janani, L., Rahimi-Movaghar, A., Rajabi, Z., Rahmani, A., Hojati, Z., Khalagi, K., & Motevalian, S. A. (2021). Validity of self-reported substance use: Research setting versus primary health care setting. *Substance Abuse Treatment, Prevention, and Policy*, *16*(1), 66. https://doi.org/10.1186/s13011-021-00398-3

Lane, D. C., & DeCamp, W. (2017). "Sports will keep 'em out of trouble": A comparative analysis of substance use among adolescents and young adults. *Journal of Sport and Health Research*, *9*(1), 41–52.

Lentillon-Kaestner, V., & Ohl, F. (2011). Can we measure accurately the prevalence of doping? *Scandinavian Journal of Medicine & Science in Sports*, *21*(6), e132–e142. https://doi.org/10.1111/j.1600-0838.2010.01199.x

Lisha, N. E., & Sussman, S. (2010). Relationship of high school and college sports participation with alcohol, tobacco, and illicit drug use: A review. *Addictive Behaviors*, *35*(5), 399–407. https://doi.org/10.1016/j.addbeh.2009.12.032

Magura, S., Laudet, A., & Goldberger, B. A. (Eds.). (1999). Improving the validity of behavioral drug abuse research through drug testing. In *Drug testing technology*. CRC Press.

Martin, T. M. (2021). *2021 Public report of major league baseball's joint drug prevention and treatment program*. Major League Baseball, Joint Drug Prevention and Treatment Program. https://img.mlbstatic.com/mlb-images/image/upload/mlb/lzxuuz0tl35vonqzjruc.pdf

McVeigh, J., Hearne, E., Boardley, I., Bates, G., Hope, V., Ralphs, R., & Van Hout, M. C. (2021). Generating evidence on the use of Image and performance enhancing drugs in the UK: Results from a scoping review and expert consultation by the anabolic steroid UK network. *Harm Reduction Journal*, *18*(1), 107. https://doi.org/10.1186/s12954-021-00550-z

National Collegiate Athletic Association. (2018). *NCAA national study on substance use habits of college student-athletes*.

Pate, R. R., Trost, S. G., Levin, S., & Dowda, M. (2000). Sports participation and health-related behaviors among U.S. youth. *Archives of Pediatrics & Adolescent Medicine*, *154*(9), 904. https://doi.org/10.1001/archpedi.154.9.904

Peretti-Watel, P., & Lorente, F. O. (2004). Cannabis use, sport practice and other leisure activities at the end of adolescence. *Drug and Alcohol Dependence*, *73*(3), 251–257. https://doi.org/10.1016/j.drugalcdep.2003.10.016

Rasmussen, N. (2008). America's first amphetamine epidemic 1929–1971. *American Journal of Public Health*, *98*(6), 974–985. https://doi.org/10.2105/AJPH.2007.110593

Reuter, P., Caulkins, J. P., & Midgette, G. (2021). Heroin use cannot be measured adequately with a general population survey. *Addiction*, *116*(10), 2600–2609. https://doi.org/10.1111/add.15458

Sagoe, D., McVeigh, J., Bjørnebekk, A., Essilfie, M.-S., Andreassen, C. S., & Pallesen, S. (2015). Polypharmacy among anabolic-androgenic steroid users: A descriptive metasynthesis.

Substance Abuse Treatment, Prevention, and Policy, *10*, 12. https://doi.org/10.1186/s13011-015-0006-5

Salinas, M., Floodgate, W., & Ralphs, R. (2019). Polydrug use and polydrug markets amongst image and performance enhancing drug users: Implications for harm reduction interventions and drug policy. *International Journal of Drug Policy*, *67*, 43–51. https://doi.org/10.1016/j.drugpo.2019.01.019

Severson, H. H., Klein, K., Lichtenstein, E., Kaufman, N., & Orleans, C. T. (2005). Smokeless tobacco use among professional baseball players: Survey results, 1998 to 2003. *Tobacco Control*, *14*(1), 31–36. https://doi.org/10.1136/tc.2004.007781

Skarberg, K., Nyberg, F., & Engstrom, I. (2009). Multisubstance use as a feature of addiction to anabolic-androgenic steroids. *European Addiction Research*, *15*(2), 99–106. https://doi.org/10.1159/000199045

Thevis, M. (2008). Determination of the prevalence of anabolic steroids, stimulants, and selected drugs subject to doping controls among elite sport students using analytical chemistry. *Journal of Sports Sciences*, *26*(10), 1059–1065. https://pubmed.ncbi.nlm.nih.gov/18608840/

Turnock, L. A. (2021). Polydrug use and drug market intersections within powerlifting cultures in remote South-West England. *Performance Enhancement & Health*, *8*(4), 100186. https://doi.org/10.1016/j.peh.2021.100186

UFC Anti-Doping Program. (2021). *Testing numbers*. https://ufc.usada.org/testing/results/testing-numbers/

U.S. Anti-Doping Agency. (2020, March 17). *USADA statement regarding COVID-19 and anti-doping testing protocol*. https://www.usada.org/statement/usada-statement-covid19-antidoping-protocol/

U.S. Department of Health and Human Services, Substance Abuse and Mental Health Services Administration, Center for Behavioral Health Statistics and Quality. (2016). *National survey on drug use and health, 2016*. RTI International [distributor].

U.S. Department of Health and Human Services, Substance Abuse and Mental Health Services Administration, Center for Behavioral Health Statistics and Quality. (2018). *National survey on drug use and health, 2018*. Substance Abuse and Mental Health Services Administration. https://datafiles.samhsa.gov/

U.S. Department of Health and Human Services, Substance Abuse and Mental Health Services Administration, Center for Behavioral Health Statistics and Quality. (2020). *National survey on drug use and health 2020*. Substance Abuse and Mental Health Services Administration. https://datafiles.samhsa.gov/

Van de Ven, K., Maher, L., Wand, H., Memedovic, S., Jackson, E., & Iversen, J. (2018). Health risk and health seeking behaviours among people who inject performance and image enhancing drugs who access needle syringe programs in Australia. *Drug and Alcohol Review*, *37*(7), 837–846. https://doi.org/10.1111/dar.12831

van de Ven, K., & Mulrooney, K. J. D. (2017). Social suppliers: Exploring the cultural contours of the performance and image enhancing drug (PIED) market among bodybuilders in the Netherlands and Belgium. *International Journal of Drug Policy*, *40*, 6–15. https://doi.org/10.1016/j.drugpo.2016.07.009

Veliz, P., Epstein-Ngo, Q. M., Meier, E., Ross-Durow, P. L., McCabe, S. E., & Boyd, C. J. (2014). Painfully obvious: A longitudinal examination of medical use and misuse of opioid medication among adolescent sports participants. *Journal of Adolescent Health*, *54*(3), 333–340. https://doi.org/10.1016/j.jadohealth.2013.09.002

Veliz, P. T., Boyd, C., & McCabe, S. E. (2013). Playing through pain: Sports participation and nonmedical use of opioid medications among adolescents. *American Journal of Public Health*, *103*(5), e28–e30. https://doi.org/10.2105/AJPH.2013.301242

Wichstrøm, T., & Wichstrøm, L. (2009). Does sports participation during adolescence prevent later alcohol, tobacco and cannabis use? *Addiction*, *104*(1), 138–149. https://doi.org/10.1111/j.1360-0443.2008.02422.x

World Anti-Doping Agency. (2013). *2013 Anti-doping testing figures*.

World Anti-Doping Agency. (2014). *2014 Anti-doping testing figures*.

World Anti-Doping Agency. (2015). *2015 Anti-doping testing figures*.

World Anti-Doping Agency. (2016). *2016 Anti-doping testing figures*.

World Anti-Doping Agency. (2017). *2017 Anti-doping testing figures*.

World Anti-Doping Agency. (2018). *2018 Anti-doping testing figures*.

World Anti-Doping Agency. (2019). *2019 Anti-doping testing figures*.

World Anti-Doping Agency. (2020). *2020 Anti-doping testing figures*. https://www.wada-ama.org/sites/default/files/2022-01/2020_anti-doping_testing_figures_en.pdf

Yusko, D. A., Buckman, J. F., White, H. R., & Pandina, R. J. (2008). Alcohol, Tobacco, illicit drugs, and performance enhancers: A comparison of use by college student athletes and nonathletes. *Journal of American College Health, 57*(3), 281–290. https://doi.org/10.3200/JACH.57.3.281-290

Zahnow, R., McVeigh, J., Bates, G., Hope, V., Kean, J., Campbell, J., & Smith, J. (2018). Identifying a typology of men who use anabolic androgenic steroids (AAS). *International Journal of Drug Policy, 55*, 105–112. https://doi.org/10.1016/j.drugpo.2018.02.022

CHAPTER 3

Theories of Psychoactive Substance Use in Sport

In recent decades, two primary narratives have emerged to make sense of doping, or IPED use, among elite athletes; individuals so exposed are generally talked about as either ruthlessly ambitious masterminds or reluctant victims, compelled to contaminate their bodies in pursuit of team, or national, greatness. Reportage on American cyclist Lance Armstrong perhaps best exemplifies the former storyline, with even the *New York Times* characterizing the 7-time Tour de France champion as an "infamous cheat, a defiant liar, and a bully" (Macur, 2012). By contrast, Russian participants in a vast system of state-sponsored doping were labeled "pawns in a broken and corrupt system" by the International Paralympic Committee Athletes' Council (Nicholson, n.d.). Ten years later, such an understanding prevailed when allegations of child abuse accompanied public revelations of a positive doping test for the Russian Olympic Committee's star figure skater, Kamila Valieva (Abad-Santos, 2022). Typically, neither frame—athlete as villain or victim—considers the dynamic between individual behavior and the sports environment, or approaches doping as a rational or legible decision shaped by situational risks and rewards.

A similar critique might be levied against popular representations of psychoactive drug use among sports figures, when such understanding is attempted at all. In an era where the boundaries between news, sports, and entertainment have evaporated, accounts often focus on the individual athlete ("tragic") and the drug(s) (mythically powerful), while the complex circumstances that led to their connection are neglected (see, for example, Lemoncelli, 2021). In some instances, the rapidly expanding science around chronic traumatic encephalopathy (CTE)—a degenerative brain condition linked to repetitive head injury—has been used to fill in blanks; characterized by emotional volatility, aggression, and impulse control problems, CTE has also been cited in the development of SUD among football, hockey, and other contact sport athletes (Mayo Clinic, n.d.). Where biological factors certainly play a role in many patterns of drug use, commentators too often fail to consider their interplay with other aspects of biography and social context. Not only do we struggle to escape the prism of performance enhancement, but it is rare that influences outside prominent athletes' sports careers are considered. Expelled from the 2021 U.S. Olympic team after testing positive for tetrahydrocannabinol (THC), sprinter Sha'Carri Richardson spoke about the death of her mother only weeks before, tweeting simply, "I am human" (Weisholtz, 2021).

In focusing on substance use in this particular population, this chapter will look to sports participation as a factor that shapes drug initiation, patterns of use, associated harms—and benefits (with the exception of performance-enhancing effects, which are beyond the scope of this text). Athletic participation often functions as a type of social or professional membership with implications for one's socioeconomic status, social network, and lifestyle. For this reason, we will largely review different sociological and psychosocial theories of substance use that speak to, but also extend beyond, athletes. While not honed in the study of athletes specifically, these theories may nevertheless illuminate how sports participation factors as both "risk" and "protective" factor for different kinds of drug use, recalling the epidemiology discussed in Chapter 2. The chapter will conclude with an extended application of "risk environment" theory to psychoactive drug use in sport (Rhodes, 2009). A heuristic that accounts for not only the likelihood of drug initiation but also patterns of harmful drug use, risk environment theory conceptualizes different kinds of drug-related risk, shaped by different levels and spheres of social life (peer group, neighborhood, health systems, law enforcement, etc.). Crucially, this framework requires us to consider how sport and team environments are themselves shaped externally by culture, law, and policy, thus implying multiple points of intervention for the reduction of drug-related harms. Moreover, by charting unique confluences of drug policy, medical care, and sport subcultures, risk environment theory allows us to understand substance use trajectories that are specific to athletes.

The Resonance of Athletic and Drug "Careers" Over the Life Course

While this chapter is predicated on the idea that sports participation may be salient to individuals' use of different psychoactive drugs, we must first acknowledge that this will not always be true. In other words, one person's athletic history may hold little relevance for their uptake and continued consumption of certain substances, while this particular biographical fact may be highly consequential for another person's drug career. Put another way, athletes may use psychoactive substances for the same general reasons as nonathletes: experimentation; socialization; self-medication (for stress, physical pain, or emotional distress); enhancement of energy, alertness, and self-confidence; the pursuit of pleasure or the alleviation of boredom (McDuff et al.,

2019; McDuff & Baron, 2005). It is possible, however, that some of these universal motivations may arise more frequently or more intensely within the context of an athletic "career"—a commonly used word with a second sociological meaning.

In everyday parlance, the term "career" is usually applied to employment, or the series of paid positions one holds over the lifetime, typically in the same field of practice, with the expectation of increases in salary or status. Within sociological theory, the careers concept is used more generally to understand individuals' progression, or regression, within different social spheres, including but exceeding occupation. For example, the progression of disease and illness, the transition from juvenile delinquency to adult criminality, and the escalation of drug use have all been analyzed through the lens of "careers" (see, for example, Becker, 1997; Elder & Pavalko, 1993; Goffman, 1961; Perry & Pescosolido, 2012; Pescosolido, 1992; Xia et al., 2015). Looking at drug use specifically, careers theory has characterized common stages of substance use—initiation, escalation, maintenance, and desistance—which individuals may progress through dynamically, moving both forward and backward and repeating or stalling at different points in the sequence (Coombs, 1981)

If we consider substance use and athletic careers in tandem, it is easy to see how the evolution of the former may be affected by the latter (as well as the reverse). Perhaps most obviously, the advancement of one's athletic career may be contingent on the initiation and calculated escalation of drug use, for reasons of not only performance enhancement but also pain management (Bents et al., 2004; Cottler et al., 2011). Drug initiation—or first use—may also follow from social initiation within a particular sport or team milieu, requiring the internalization of peer norms around substance use, or simply acquaintance with someone who can supply; a wealth of research conducted with both athletes and nonathletes has demonstrated, for example, that a majority of individuals who report NUPO acquire them from friends or family, not from doctors (see, for example, Cottler et al., 2011; Ford et al., 2020). A topic that will be discussed in more detail in subsequent sections, psychoactive substance use may serve as a means of managing the stress that accompanies that coordination of multiple social careers (athletic, academic, professional, personal, drug). Finally, prior studies have also shown how substance use waxes and wanes alongside the seasonal patterns of sports involvement, with psychoactive drug consumption shown to rise two- to fourfold in the off-season (Yusko et al., 2008). Some kinds of substance use may enhance the mundane events that characterize the athletic lifestyle, allowing for cathartic celebration in the aftermath of a win, commiseration following a loss, or the passage of time during a long game (Walters et al., 2021).

In positing a prime window, and average duration, for drug use careers, research in this vein reveals another way in which drug use and sports participation overlap; namely, both "careers" begin, in seriousness, in adolescence, peak in young adulthood, and gradually decline thereafter. A classic study of illicit opioid users concluded that individuals "matured out" of their drug careers, on average, by age 31—the same age at which a 2020 study concluded that elite Olympic team athletes retire from sport (Lopez de Subijana et al., 2020; Winick, 1962). It is here that life-course theories of drug use can help us make further sense of both sports and substance use career trajectories. In addition to mapping the ways in which deviance, or behavior that transgresses social norms, ebbs and flows with age, life-course theories suggest that such careers are often shaped by "turning points"—important events that trigger the intensification, reduction, or cessation of the behavior in question. Traditionally, important turning points arrive in the period between young adulthood and early-middle age (e.g., high school and college graduation, full-time employment, marriage, and parenthood) and may thus explain the diminution of drug use during this life stage. As individuals take on increasing responsibilities, and enter into new social networks, psychoactive substance use may no longer fit into their routine.

Similarly, the "turning point" of athletic retirement, whether due to physical decline or school graduation, may represent the effective end of some substance use patterns, which no longer make sense outside of competitive training or team bonding. Interestingly, data on AAS use among U.S. adolescents and young adults may illustrate how athletic career "turning points" may promote drug desistance. Annual numbers from the "Monitoring the Future" survey shows that roughly 1.1% of American 12th graders self-reported AAS use in 2017, a figure nearly threefold that of National Collegiate Athletic Association (NCAA) (college) survey participants, at 0.4% (Johnston et al., 2018; NCAA, 2018). One interpretation of this discrepancy is that high school graduation (and/or college matriculation) denotes important turning points for sports involvement, and related drug use. While many individuals may conclude their athletic careers in high school ("retirement"), others may pursue a higher level of competition in college (and, in turn, face sanction for banned substance use). At the same time, turning points may be bidirectional, with substance use increasing or decreasing in their aftermath, depending on other life circumstances and larger social structures (Waldorf et al., 1991). Where an individual might decide to discontinue drinking in college in order to maximize their athletic performance, the finality of this decision is likely to be swayed by peer or team norms around alcohol consumption. Moreover, to paraphrase the drugs researcher Philip Jenkins (1999), "when one drug door closes, another always opens." National survey data indicates that AAS use falls off after high school, but among student-athletes specifically, other kinds of psychoactive and performance-enhancing drug may take off. As a turning point, college enrollment may imply escalation, not abstinence, from certain kinds of drug use. Moreover, nearly every kind of (measured) substance use increases alongside class standing, or college year, with seniors "besting" freshman in every drug category with the exception of e-cigarettes (NCAA, 2018). Finally, it might be noted that elite athletic careers often imply the deferral of conventional turning points in adulthood, such as marriage, parenthood, or stable employment. Although there is little data to suggest that high-performance athletes engage in above-average levels of substance use, it is possible that fewer "social investments"—a partner, child, or permanent career—may promote longer-term dependence for those who do (for a discussion on the progression of athletic careers and personal "turning points," see Wylleman et al., 2012).

"The Ethic of Sport" and Socialization Theories of Drug Use

As mentioned previously, major biographical turning points are thought to shape drug use by shifting individuals' social roles, responsibilities, and milieu—the people that surround us in our daily life, whose actions and values we try to model. These pivotal life events are usually seen as dampening deviance, as accomplishments such as marriage, child-bearing, hiring, or a promotion tend to increase one's stakes in conventional behavior and erode ties with nonconformist company (key tenets of social control theory also, discussed in the next section). However, some transitions may in fact increase one's exposure to individuals who use psychoactive substances—and, depending on the particular group and its meaning, socialization into these subcultures may be hard to resist. Socialization theories of substance use highlight the influence of one's social network on the uptake of different drugs, as well as patterns of consumption over time. While myriad theories in sociology and psychology fall under this umbrella, they all assert two basic principles: (1) drug use (and other forms of illicit activity) is learned behavior; (2) these behaviors are more likely to be learned from close social contacts (Bandura et al., 1961; Burgess & Akers, 1966; Cressey, 1960; Sutherland, 1947).

It is perhaps differential association theory that best illustrates the processes by which substance use is learned within the context of sport (Sutherland, 1947). Sutherland's theory locates the lynchpin of deviant behavior within the company one keeps, the "associations" who may explicitly or implicitly encourage antisocial sentiments and actions. Within such interactions, "instruction" is twofold, conveying both the logistics of prohibited behaviors, as well as messages that support their enactment. In other words, one must learn both the motivations for and techniques of criminality. Sutherland notes that the transmission of deviant behavior is contingent on the nature of the social contact and varies alongside "frequency, duration, priority, and intensity"; we are more likely to effectively absorb "definitions favorable to the violation of the law" from esteemed individuals we connect with often, for sustained periods—a qualification that most certainly applies to athletic peers and teammates. Winnowing our focus to illegal, banned, or harmful patterns of substance use, the "technical" aspects of these activities may not be immediately obvious, especially when considering the most banal manifestations, such as drinking. Alcohol use, however, is perhaps the most clear-cut application of differential association theory within this topic, with multiple studies demonstrating the importance of team attachment or attraction, and the perception of team norms favorable to drinking, as key drivers for athletes' personal consumption (Exner et al., 2021; Graupensperger et al., 2020; Grossbard et al., 2009; Wechsler et al., 1997). Teammates' habits (descriptive norms) and perceived dis/approval (injunctive norms) around drinking may be the most important facets of this "hidden curriculum," although it may be said that specific alcohol preferences and preparations are learned in these actions as well. With regard to other drugs, such as marijuana or injectable substances, techniques of administration may have to be more explicitly taught. (Anyone, who has read in-depth reportage on blood doping practices within Lance Armstrong's Post Service cycling team knows the astonishing complexity of such regimes.) Indeed, differential association has demonstrated relevance to many types of drug use in sport; other studies of elite and college athletes have shown that "knowing other athletes who use illicit drugs" was among the most significant predictors of this behavior, while playing a team (versus an individual) sport additionally elevates risk (Dunn, 2011; Wechsler et al., 1997).

Of course, the norms and values one learns within a team are not necessarily pathological, even when they have the effect of encouraging drug use. In fact, several authors have framed athletes' consumption of psychoactive substances as reflecting their commitment to the "ethic of sport," a set of subcultural "rules" that define membership on a team and/or identity as an athlete. As elaborated by Hughes and Coakley (1991), the demands of this "ethic" are fourfold: (1) real athletes place the demands of their sport above everything else; (2) they will always strive for perfection; (3) athletes accept the inherent risk of injury, which will not deter them from competition; and (4) they recognize no obstacles or limitations in their pursuit of victory, whether individual or team (see also Ford et al., 2018). It is straightforward to see how subscription to the sport ethic may justify the use of IPED, which may be understood as necessary tools to push past training plateaus. However, returning to the third of the precepts outlined previously, athletes' nonmedical consumption of POs can also be understood through this rubric; in fact, the use of diverse drugs for pain management may reflect a dogged orientation to athletic achievement, even if such practices occur outside of medical supervision. A prohibited behavior that results from "overconformity"—or enthusiastic adherence—to an ethic that is generally praised within society at large, substance use in sport has been labeled as a form of "positive deviance." (Arguably, positive deviance may also have beneficial effects. Anecdotal evidence suggests that a majority of professional hockey and football players, in the NHL and NFL respectively, consume marijuana as a means of relieving pain and avoiding more potent analgesics, such as opioids. While transgressing league rules and federal laws, this practice may reduce the risk of medication dependence and overdose for individual athletes, while promoting the normalization of medical cannabis in society at large [Newsham, 2021].)

These theories focus largely on the sway of athletes' peers/teammates on the adoption of views favorable to substance use, but, of course, other actors wield influence in this sphere of decision-making. Research on adolescents' experimentation with psychoactive drugs has specifically highlighted the role of parents in discouraging teenagers' progression to regular drug use, or illicit drug use after earlier experiences with alcohol and tobacco. Most famously, Kandel et al.'s (1978) work on stages of substance use among secondary school students identified the quality of parent–teen relationships as a key factor mediating the move from marijuana to other illegal drugs. Such findings on parental influence have been replicated among college student-athletes, showing that parents' explicit communication of consequences related to drinking reduced alcohol use in the first year of university; former high school coaches may exert similar influence on new college students' drinking volume (Mastroleo et al., 2012; Turrisi et al., 2009). Moreover, while parental messaging around alcohol may represent a counterweight to peer norms (observed or inferred), parents (and coaches) may facilitate the development of coping skills among student-athletes, which, in turn, deter overconsumption of psychoactive substances (Tamminen & Holt, 2012).

It might be noted that Kandel's (1975) work on stages of adolescent substance use is best known for its conceptualization of marijuana as a gateway drug. In other words, individuals' use of marijuana is significantly associated with subsequent use of other illicit drugs, even after accounting for other explanatory variables. Even while the mechanisms—social, psychological, or biological—that underlie this transition are still poorly characterized, the gateway hypothesis has nevertheless been applied to other substance use sequences, such as the initiation of cigarette smoking among adolescents who vape, the uptake of illicit drugs among athletes who consume IPED, and participation in doping by nutritional supplement users (Arvary & Pope, 2000; Backhouse et al., 2013; Mendelsohn & Hall, 2020). As with marijuana, the status of IPED, and AAS specifically, as substances that encourage progression to "harder" psychoactive substances is disputed in the literature and not consistently supported by existing evidence. Cross-sectional analyses do indicate that athletes who have used IPED, and AAS in particular, are more likely to have also consumed marijuana, cocaine, illicit psychedelics, and (unprescribed) opioids, amphetamines, and benzodiazepines, compared to athletes without IPED experience (Buckman et al., 2009; Garevik & Rane, 2010; Skarberg et al., 2009). Similarly, multiple studies have determined that athletes who consume nutritional supplements also report higher levels of doping, or more positive attitudes toward IPED (Backhouse et al., 2013; Barkoukis et al., 2015; Hurst et al., 2021). However, studies showing that AAS use typically precedes "general illicit drug" use are scant, confined to small, in-treatment research samples, and contradicted by research that demonstrates the inverse pathway, deficiencies that also characterize research around the "supplement gateway" (Backhouse et al., 2013; Kanayama et al., 2003; Skarberg et al., 2009). Nevertheless, several studies have illuminated plausible mechanisms for co-use of IPED and illicit psychoactive substances. Where some have suggested that illicit drugs with analgesic properties (e.g., marijuana, opioids) might ameliorate the unpleasant side effects of AAS use, other researchers assert a sociological connection, with users sourcing both psychoactive and performance-enhancing drugs from illicit markets (Parrett, 2010; Salinas et al., 2019; Striegel et al., 2006). Overall, however, the gateway hypothesis has failed to generate compelling evidence of a neurological link between different kinds of drug use; in other words, no human subjects studies have determined that marijuana, AAS, or nutritional supplements "prime" the brain to crave other psychoactive substances. Moreover, confirmatory studies frequently fail to test for confounding variables that may explain both initial and subsequent types of drug use, such as family and peer substance use, mental health diagnoses, or education (Degenhardt et al., 2010; Etter, 2018; Kim & Selya, 2020; Mendelsohn & Hall, 2020).

Stress, Self-medication, and Structural Theories of Athlete Drug Use

Truthfully, structural, and structural–functionalist, explanations of athletes' substance use have already been conjured as part of previous discussions concerning group norms, the subculture of sport, "positive deviance," and drug consumption as a coping mechanism. A diverse pot of theories spanning three centuries, structural/functionalist accounts of deviance tend to implicate the larger cultural, economic, and political sphere—"social structure"—not unlike the risk environment theory that follows. To acknowledge the untidiness of this chapter's organization is to acknowledge the artificiality of all these intellectual groupings; certainly, basic sociological precepts are shared among many of these theoretical schools, which fundamentally recognize substance use as a phenomenon best elucidated at the level of social groups. A defining feature of structuralist theories is their investment in social stability and assumption of the functional interdependence of existing social institutions and social roles. For this reason, some manifestations of deviance, or nonnormative beliefs and behavior, are supposed to serve a positive function within the maintenance of social cohesion, albeit for reasons that are not immediately intuitive. The forefather of structural-functionalism, Émile Durkheim (1951), posited that deviant actions and individuals helped to illuminate the norms they transgress, in turn reifying the boundaries of acceptable behavior and consolidating the conformist social identity of rule-abiding actors. His principal 20th-century inheritor, Talcott Parsons, went so far as to identify formal deviant social roles, a theoretical pirouette that effectively neutralizes the social threat of transgressive behavior by assimilating it into normal patterns of interaction.

In his most famous work, however, Durkheim (1951) also acknowledged that social deviance could surpass healthy levels, a trend he framed as symptomatic of deep social pathology, or a society in distress. Writing himself during a period of stark social churn, he coined a unique term for a context characterized by rapid, destructive change, resulting in a chaos of behavioral norms:

anomie. In fin-de-siècle France, anomie was wrought by the overlapping effects of industrialization, urbanization, and political revolution, social forces that Durkheim correlated with the national epidemiology of suicide (as well as divorce). But anomie is a wonderfully flexible and scalable concept, which may also describe the initiation and escalation of drug use within any environment characterized by ambiguous rules, low social control, and newly atomized individuals: criteria that apply to a 19th-century tenement, or the first week of university. Research discussed previously has already established college as a space and time defined by elevated levels of alcohol consumption, with risk further heightened by participation in some sports. Such behavior may reflect a ritual of team bonding, an appropriate expression of age, or a response to conflicting rules and disintegrating norms by young people living away from home for the first time. As Dunn and Wang (2003) concluded in a study of physical activity and substance use among university students, "…the college years are usually a time of experimentation and freedom away from parental influence." Ford (2007) also does well to characterize the normative chaos experienced by college students, explaining that freshmen may be especially susceptible to following the substance use practices of their new teammates, as their "normative guidelines from the past" may no longer be relevant. Moreover, anomic drug use among athletes may not be limited to college; we might also frame the transition from amateur to professional athletic competition as a time defined by new networks, new expectations, and new rules, formal and informal. A societal designation in Durkheim's work, the anomie concept still conjures the stress felt by individuals, and, in fact, extensions of anomie theory focused more on its psychological dimensions and behavioral consequences.

Robert K. Merton (1938) described anomie in terms that resonate starkly with the pressures felt by high-performance athletes—as a psychic conflict that results from the cultural (or subcultural) imperative to attain wealth and status, in the face of structural conditions that prevent most individuals from succeeding via legal or "institutionalized" routes. Merton's theory was based on his observation that the so-called "American Dream" was out of reach for most citizens, stymied by structural inequalities that did not simply yield to hard work and ambition. Confronted with the hopelessness of their situation, individuals might take four paths: (1) continue trying, and believing (conformists); (2) go through the motions, while accepting their futility (ritualists); (3) give up all pretense of effort and faith (retreatists); or (4) adopt unsanctioned means of achieving their goal (innovators). For Merton, these final two "adaptations" implied a turn to deviance, as individuals tried to "escape" from their situation through the pursuit of oblivion—often substance use—or chased money, fame, and power by breaking the rules. Turning to elite or professional sports, it is easy to see how success in athletics represents a subset of, or perhaps path to, the American Dream. Champion athletes often become general celebrities, additionally drawing impressive salaries, endorsement deals, and opportunities to parlay their physical prowess into long-lasting security. Unfortunately, elite sport is, more often than not, a zero-sum game. There can only be a small pool of winners, and victory is conditioned by physical, social, and economic advantages that are not evenly distributed. In other words, practice, discipline, and determination do not inevitably lead to triumph; adjuvants may be required. When discussing deviant "innovation" in sport, IPED quickly come to mind. Importantly, Merton's theory helps us understand how individuals who use IPED (including psychoactive substances like amphetamines) are hardly the antisocial villains we so often imagine. Instead, they may be seen as among the most ardent adherents to a high stakes subculture that demands total devotion. Reflecting on liminal forms of drug use in sport, such as PO overconsumption, it may, in fact, be hard to draw a solid line between conformists and innovators.

Where Merton's depiction of dependent drug users as "retreatists" has been thoroughly critiqued as inaccurate and offensive, the idea that many individuals consume psychoactive substances to mediate stress, frustration, and disappointment is largely a matter of cultural commonsense, as well as a conclusion consonant with general strain theory (Agnew & White, 1992). For Robert Agnew (1992), "strain" is a frequent result of thwarted expectations, or a disjuncture between aspirations and actual outcomes; furthermore, this subjective distress may be magnified by perceived injustice, or the belief that others have unfairly undermined one's chances of success. In the wake of this revelation, individuals, and particularly young people, may turn to delinquency and/or drug use to achieve other goals, feel rewarded or respected, or simply evade negative feelings. Multiple authors have explored athletes' use of psychoactive substances as a form of psychological self-medication that specifically treats the erosion of their sporting ambitions, difficulty managing multiple realms of social expectation, or tense relationships within or outside their sports life (Denham, 2014; Heyman, 1986). Indeed, the myriad strains encountered by athletes at all levels have been well cataloged, with Arnold and Fletcher (2012) identifying thirty-four distinct "organizational stressors" across four broad categories, including "Leadership and Personnel Issues" and "Cultural and Team Issues." Interestingly, this work identifies a number of negative interactions that may emerge as a result of athletic involvement and that in turn, cause strain (and possibly, drug use). By contrast, a final structural theory of substance use points to sport as a venue that encourages positive relationships with conventional actors whose influence deters deviant behavior on the balance.

Social control theories understand individuals' tendency toward deviance as a function of their bond to society; as the strength of the social bond increases, the likelihood of antisocial behavior, such as drug use, falls. As conceptualized by Travis Hirschi (1969), the social bond is comprised of four elements, or mechanisms, of control, all of which may be illustrated with specific reference to sport, as a conventional institution that encourages normative behavior. First, "attachment" to others implies the internalization of and adherence to shared norms. If an individual perceives their teammates to disapprove of substance use, it is less likely they will engage in this negatively sanctioned pastime. "Commitment" to a line of conventional action—for example, playing on an elite team, or qualification for a high-performance competition—implies the avoidance of activities that might threaten continued membership or success. Serious athletes may be unwilling to compromise their sports careers for short-term pleasure. According to Hirschi, "involvement" with prosocial activities may logistically negate opportunities for deviant behavior; after training, practicing, and competing, little time (and energy) may be left over for the pursuit of drinking or drug use. Finally, to belong to a conventional social group or institution is to "believe" in the values that deter deviance. If athletes are less likely to consume illicit drugs, it is because they judge this behavior to be inherently wrong or harmful.

Multiple contemporary researchers have applied social control theory to explain the protective effects of sport against some forms of substance use. However, it has to be more complicated. Showing significantly lower odds of all forms of psychoactive substance use among high school sports participants compared to their nonathlete peers, Pate et al. (2000) considered several ways in which sports may fortify adolescents' social bond, identifying the cultural norms associated with such programs, their emphasis on "personal health and fitness as prerequisites to optimal performance," and the deviant opportunity costs of athletic involvement. Ford (2008) further posits the greater "stake in conformity" felt by college student-athletes, who were shown to engage in relatively reduced levels of nonmedical prescription drug use. Finally, others see the tenets of control theory validated in survey data revealing "fear of getting drug tested" or perceived harm to "athletic performance" as major disincentives to substance use among college student-athletes (NCAA, 2018). Of course, data on the deterrent impact of drug testing is notoriously inconsistent, with several studies showing no effects among student-athletes (Goldberg et al., 2007; Yamaguchi et al., 2003).

At the same time, such applications of social control theory are specific to illicit drug use; the protective effect of sport appears notably absent in other studies of alcohol consumption patterns among young athletes. However, social control theory has also been mobilized to elucidate the elevated risk of binge drinking within older student-athlete populations. Confirming college athletes' increased propensity for alcohol consumption, Lane and DeCamp (2017) frame this finding as perfectly consonant with control theory, with the caveat that attachment to university sports teams may produce conformity to unhealthy behaviors. Similarly, Zhou et al. (2016) suggest that "sport-related drinking may be an avenue for building group identification." The normalization of certain kinds of substance use within the general population, among young people, or within athletic subcultures, in particular, may also undercut the effects of "attachment." For example, steadily increasing levels of cannabis use and availability have combined with (or encouraged) more liberal attitudes and policies around the drug, with many governments and institutions relaxing or eliminating cannabis prohibitions; it is hardly surprising, then, that cannabis consumption is increasingly destigmatized within sport (Parker et al., 2002; Reid, 2020; Sznitman & Taubman, 2016). Likewise, research among athletes who use IPED have highlighted the social component of such practices, with such athletes' peers, coaches, and other team members representing crucial supports for doping; within subcultures in which IPED are normalized, such as some bodybuilding communities, use and distribution signifies a strong attachment to, and successful socialization within, the sport (Pappa & Kennedy, 2013; van de Ven & Mulrooney, 2017). Some scholars have gone so far as to identify IPED use as a "cultural heritage" within some sports, with doping only transformed into a social problem with the advent of antidoping legislation. Ohl et al. (2015) specifically examine doping as a cultural practice within elite cycling, which is embedded in the collaborative "production of performance" by not only athletes, but their coaches, trainers, and physicians, among others. In such cases, participation in doping may represent not deviation from but conformity to a sport culture that has been shaped by complex historical, economic, and social forces and that is constantly reproduced through interaction. Seen in this light, the use of IPED represents much more than a rational desire to win and profit; instead, it becomes an expression of adherence to formal or informal work group expectations and a result of socialization with older, established peers. Sport subcultures that are defined by doping may produce dissonant effects on athlete identity, as individuals must reconcile the stigmatization of IPED in society at large, with their valuation inside their team or sport (Ohl et al., 2015).

Understanding Unique Substance Use Pathways in Sport: Risk Environment Theory

Arguably, all of the theories presented previously may be useful in elucidating different kinds of substance use among different athlete demographics; indeed, we should consider this diverse pool of heuristics to be complementary, further allowing us to relate athletic involvement to other social variables that predict, or protect against, deviance. Still, sport may also shape some unique pathways in psychoactive substance use that are more difficult to trace using general criminological or sociological explanations. Moreover, athletes' substance use careers may be molded at multiple levels, by factors both internal and external to sport, in ways that further reflect the shifting significance of sport within larger local, national, and global cultures. The theory of risk environments is introduced here as a framework that effectively captures the complex interplay of team dynamics, institutional subcultures, national drug policy, and sport-centric societies in incentivizing certain kinds of use among athletes, with disparate risks—and rewards. As written by Rhodes (2002, p. 88), "risk environment" refers to the "space—whether social or physical—in which a variety of factors interact to increase the chances of drug related harms." Drug-related risk, which is itself conceptualized across a number of dimensions (medical, psychological, social, economic, legal), is the product of multiple environments interacting at both the (micro) level of milieu and (macro) social structures. Table 1 adapts Rhodes' original illustration of nested risk and enabling environments to identify factors specific to sport.

Table 1: Risk and Enabling Environment for Psychoactive Drug Use in Sport

	Micro	**Macro**
Physical	Secret sites of drug use (e.g., dorm rooms, hotels)	Drug trafficking routes
	Public sites of drug use (e.g., gyms) that necessitate rushed consumption	National/international competition sites
Social	Team, sport-specific norms of drug use	Cultural norms of drug use
	Teammate, peer pressure to perform	Drug-related stigma
	Family pressure to perform	Cultural glorification of sport "celebrities"
Economic	Local access to trainer and sports medicine specialist	Access to and cost of health care
	Receipt/retention of athletic scholarships	Disproportionate economic rewards in professional sport
	Professional recruitment, income	Sport as global business
Policy	Team-level drug prohibitions and sanctions	Laws criminalizing drug use, restricting medication access
	Drug testing policies	Laws limiting access to risk reduction programs
	Institution/league/sport federation sanctions	International doping code

Table 1 identifies aspects of the athletic environment—local and large-scale—that may both motivate psychoactive substance use and perhaps heighten associated harms. Several factors included earlier may be recalled from other theories of drug use: peer norms that promote substance use as means of bonding, the strain caused by social pressure to succeed in sport, and the outsized economic rewards attached to college and professional recruitment. It might also be noted that the risk environment framework addresses substance bans and mandatory testing as policies that exacerbate drug risks. Even if such prohibitions conclusively deterred athletes' drug use, their enforcement would likely result in negative economic, social, and maybe legal consequences for athletes, an outcome that has been thoroughly detailed in applications of risk environment theory to doping (Henning et al., 2021). Here, we land at a central, simple precept of this framework, which maintains that drug-related harms are contextual—a reflection of the environments in which drugs are used, more than the nature of drugs themselves. Moreover, by demonstrating the interrelationship of different kinds of risk, this framework allows us to map drug initiation trajectories that are specific to sport.

While research has shown that relatively few individuals progress to the nonmedical use of opioid analgesics that they were formally prescribed, this "pain management" pathway may be shaped by multiple elements of the sports risk environment. Significant data does demonstrate that young adult, and many elites, athletes are at an elevated risk of injury. The NCAA injury surveillance system reports roughly 210,000 injuries among roughly 500,000 college athletes each year, while an analysis of injury trends among the top four U.S. professional sport leagues revealed over 62 injuries per 100 players (Dart, 2021; Taree et al., 2022). Injury risk may be further exacerbated by a high stakes performance environment, where team or individual success may translate into university scholarships, professional recruitment, national team qualification, or overwhelming financial rewards (Table 1). Athletes in recovery from orthopedic injury, or related surgeries, may be exposed to prescription painkillers or self-medicate with diverse substances, depending on their access to formal health care—an aspect of the economic risk environment that is additionally shaped by drug laws at different levels. In turn, athletes' pain management trajectories are influenced by social and economic imperatives to keep competing, the continued availability of their preferred drugs and the space to use them, and overlapping systems of social control. As indicated previously, the risk environment frame posits that drug-related harms often increase as access decreases; athletes who must buy, consume, and manage the effects of controlled analgesic drugs in secret are more vulnerable to medical risks (such as overdose, drug toxicity, or dependence) and, of course, negative social sanctions such as team suspension, fines, expulsion, and even arrest. Focusing on the best known category of psychoactive analgesics, POs, a handful of studies have characterized the "pain management pathway" as nonmedical use or dependence (Anthony et al., 2017; Cottler et al., 2011; Ford et al., 2018, 2020; Outlaw et al., 2018). While these studies will be explored in depth in Chapter 5, it may be noted here that they collectively highlight the impact of every aspect of the overarching sports risk environment, and thus also illuminate multiple points of intervention and risk reduction. The next chapter will also take this theoretical framework in its exploration of alcohol use among certain athlete demographics, with a specific view to elements of the social risk environment that spur some individuals to harmful patterns of drinking.

Reflection Points

1. How can we understand increases in (reported) psychoactive drug use in sport over time, despite a proliferation of anti-drug prohibition policies and laws?

2. How well do the theories discussed in this chapter explain the use of image and performance-enhancing drugs among athletes? Which theory or group of theories best applies to doping behaviors?

3. What elements of the sports "risk environment" might be modified to prevent psychoactive drug misuse or related harms?

Glossary

Anomie: A time or place characterized by rapid social change, and the breakdown of traditional norms of behavior

Deviance: A behavior or trait that is seen as violating the social norms of some group and that may be met with informal (e.g., ostracization, shaming) or formal (arrest, legal punishment) social control

Drug Careers: A concept that stipulates a predictable trajectory of drug use, from initiation, to escalation, to desistance, as well as an average duration

Norms: Rules of social behavior that are defined, explicitly or implicitly, by different social groups and enforced through positive or negative sanctions

Risk Environment: A theoretical framework that shows how drug-related risk is shaped by an individual's physical, social, economic, and policy contexts

Socialization: The process by which an individual learns the norms and values of the social groups to which they belong, typically through experiences of informal and formal social control

REFERENCES

Abad-Santos, A. (2022, February 11). *Kamila Valieva failed her drug test: Blame her coaches.* Vox. https://www.vox.com/22929275/kamila-valieva-trimetazidine-eteri-tutberidze-olympics-2022

Agnew, R. (1992). Foundation for a general strain theory of crime and delinquency. *Criminology, 30*(1), 47–88. https://doi.org/10.1111/j.1745-9125.1992.tb01093.x

Agnew, R., & White, H. R. (1992). An empirical test of general strain theory. *Criminology, 30*(4), 475–500. https://doi.org/10.1111/j.1745-9125.1992.tb01113.x

Anthony, C. A., Westermann, R. W., Bedard, N., Glass, N., Bollier, M., Hettrich, C. M., & Wolf, B. R. (2017). Opioid Demand Before and After Anterior Cruciate Ligament Reconstruction. *The American Journal of Sports Medicine, 45*(13), 3098–3103. https://doi.org/10.1177/0363546517719226

Arnold, R., & Fletcher, D. (2012). A research synthesis and taxonomic classification of the organizational stressors encountered by sport performers. *Journal of Sport and Exercise Psychology, 34*(3), 397–429. https://doi.org/10.1123/jsep.34.3.397

Arvary, D., & Pope, H. (2000). Anabolic–androgenic steroids as a gateway to opioid dependence. *New England Journal of Medicine, 342*, 1532. https://doi.org/10.1056/NEJM200005183422018

Backhouse, S. H., Whitaker, L., & Petróczi, A. (2013). Gateway to doping? Supplement use in the context of preferred competitive situations, doping attitude, beliefs, and norms. *Scandinavian Journal of Medicine & Science in Sports, 23*(2), 244–252. https://doi.org/10.1111/j.1600-0838.2011.01374.x

Bandura, A., Ross, D., & Ross, S. A. (1961). Transmission of aggression through imitation of aggressive models. *The Journal of Abnormal and Social Psychology*, *63*(3), 575–582. https://doi.org/10.1037/h0045925

Barkoukis, V., Lazuras, L., Lucidi, F., & Tsorbatzoudis, H. (2015). Nutritional supplement and doping use in sport: Possible underlying social cognitive processes. *Scandinavian Journal of Medicine & Science in Sports*, *25*(6), e582–e588. https://doi.org/10.1111/sms.12377

Becker, H. S. (1997). *Outsiders: Studies in sociology of deviance*. Free.

Bents, R. T., Tokish, J. M., & Goldberg, L. (2004). Ephedrine, pseudoephedrine, and amphetamine prevalence in college hockey players: Most report performance-enhancing use. *The Physician and Sportsmedicine*, *32*(9), 30–34. https://doi.org/10.1080/00913847.2004.11440733

Buckman, J. F., Yusko, D. A., White, H. R., & Pandina, R. J. (2009). Risk profile of male college athletes who use performance-enhancing substances. *Journal of Studies on Alcohol and Drugs*, *70*(6), 919–923. https://doi.org/10.15288/jsad.2009.70.919

Burgess, R. L., & Akers, R. L. (1966). A differential association-reinforcement theory of criminal behavior. *Social Problems*, *14*(2), 128–147. https://doi.org/10.2307/798612

Coombs, R. H. (1981). Drug abuse as career. *Journal of Drug Issues*, *11*(4), 369–387. https://doi.org/10.1177/002204268101100401

Cottler, L. B., Ben Abdallah, A., Cummings, S. M., Barr, J., Banks, R., & Forchheimer, R. (2011). Injury, pain, and prescription opioid use among former National Football League (NFL) players. *Drug and Alcohol Dependence*, *116*(1–3), 188–194. https://doi.org/10.1016/j.drugalcdep.2010.12.003

Cressey, D. R. (1960). Theory of differential association. *Social Problems*, *8*(1), 2–6.

Dart, T. (2021, September 6). College athletes are unpaid: What if injury ruins their chance of turning pro? *The Guardian*. https://www.theguardian.com/sport/2021/sep/06/college-athletes-are-unpaid-what-if-injury-ruins-their-chance-of-turning-pro

Degenhardt, L., Dierker, L., Chiu, W. T., Medina-Mora, M. E., Neumark, Y., Sampson, N., Alonso, J., Angermeyer, M., Anthony, J. C., Bruffaerts, R., de Girolamo, G., de Graaf, R., Gureje, O., Karam, A. N., Kostyuchenko, S., Lee, S., Lépine, J.-P., Levinson, D., Nakamura, Y., ... Kessler, R. C. (2010). Evaluating the drug use "gateway" theory using cross-national data: Consistency and associations of the order of initiation of drug use among participants in the WHO world mental health surveys. *Drug and Alcohol Dependence*, *108*(1), 84–97. https://doi.org/10.1016/j.drugalcdep.2009.12.001

Denham, B. E. (2014). High school sports participation and substance use: Differences by sport, race, and gender. *Journal of Child & Adolescent Substance Abuse*, *23*(3), 145–154. https://doi.org/10.1080/1067828X.2012.750974

Dunn, M. (2011). Recreational substance use among elite Australian athletes. *Drug and Alcohol Review*, *30*(1), 63–68. https://doi.org/10.1111/j.1465-3362.2010.00200.x

Dunn, M. S., & Wang, M. Q. (2003). Effects of physical activity on substance use among college students. *American Journal of Health Studies*, *18*(2/3), 126–132.

Durkheim, E. (1951). *Suicide*. The Free Press.

Elder, G. H., Jr., & Pavalko, E. K. (1993). Work careers in men's later years: Transitions, trajectories, and historical change. *Journal of Gerontology*, *48*(4), S180–S191. https://doi.org/10.1093/geronj/48.4.s180

Etter, J.-F. (2018). Gateway effects and electronic cigarettes. *Addiction*, *113*(10), 1776–1783. https://doi.org/10.1111/add.13924

Exner, J., Bitar, R., Berg, X., Pichler, E.-M., Herdener, M., Seifritz, E., & Claussen, M. C. (2021). Use of psychotropic substances among elite athletes—A narrative review. *Swiss Medical Weekly*, 151, w20412. https://doi.org/10.4414/smw.2021.20412

Ford, J. A. (2007). Substance use among college athletes: A comparison based on sport/team affiliation. *Journal of American College Health, 55*(6), 367–373. https://doi.org/10.3200/JACH.55.6.367-373

Ford, J. A. (2008). Nonmedical prescription drug use among college students: A comparison between athletes and nonathletes. *Journal of American College Health, 57*(2), 211–220. https://doi.org/10.3200/JACH.57.2.211-220

Ford, J. A., Pomykacz, C., Szalewski, A., Esteban McCabe, S., & Schepis, T. S. (2020). Friends and relatives as sources of prescription opioids for misuse among young adults: The significance of physician source and race/ethnic differences. *Substance Use & Addiction Journal, 41*(1), 93–100. https://doi.org/10.1080/08897077.2019.1635955

Ford, J. A., Pomykacz, C., Veliz, P., McCabe, S. E., & Boyd, C. J. (2018). Sports involvement, injury history, and non-medical use of prescription opioids among college students: An analysis with a national sample. *The American Journal on Addictions, 27*(1), 15–22. https://doi.org/10.1111/ajad.12657

Garevik, N., & Rane, A. (2010). Dual use of anabolic-androgenic steroids and narcotics in Sweden. *Drug and Alcohol Dependence, 109*(1–3), 144–146.

Goffman, E. (1961). *Asylums*. Anchor.

Goldberg, L., Elliot, D. L., MacKinnon, D. P., Moe, E. L., Kuehl, K. S., Yoon, M., Taylor, A., & Williams, J. (2007). Outcomes of a prospective trial of student-athlete drug testing: The student athlete testing using random notification (SATURN) study. *Journal of Adolescent Health, 41*(5), 421–429. https://doi.org/10.1016/j.jadohealth.2007.08.001

Graupensperger, S., Turrisi, R., Jones, D., & Evans, M. B. (2020). Longitudinal associations between perceptions of peer group drinking norms and students' Alcohol use frequency within college sport teams. *Alcoholism: Clinical and Experimental Research, 44*(2), 541–552. https://doi.org/10.1111/acer.14270

Grossbard, J., Hummer, J., LaBrie, J., Pederson, E., & Neighbors, C. (2009). Is substance use a team sport? Attraction to team, perceived norms, and Alcohol and Marijuana use among male and female intercollegiate athletes. *Journal of Applied Sport Psychology*, *21*(3), 247–261. https://doi.org/10.1080/10413200903019145

Henning, A., McLean, K., Andreasson, J., & Dimeo, P. (2021). Risk and enabling environments in sport: Systematic doping as harm reduction. *International Journal of Drug Policy*, *91*, 102897. https://doi.org/10.1016/j.drugpo.2020.102897

Heyman, S. R. (1986). Psychological problem patterns found with athletes. *The Clinical Psychologist*, *39*(3), 68–71.

Hirschi, T. (1969). *Causes of delinquency*. University of California Press.

Hughes, R., & Coakley, J. (1991). Positive deviance among athletes: The implications of overconformity to the sport ethic. *Sociology of Sport Journal*, *8*(4), 307–325. https://doi.org/10.1123/ssj.8.4.307

Hurst, P., Ring, C., & Kavussanu, M. (2021). Athletes using ergogenic and medical sport supplements report more favourable attitudes to doping than non-users. *Journal of Science and Medicine in Sport*, *24*(3), 307–311. https://doi.org/10.1016/j.jsams.2020.09.012

Jenkins, P. (1999). Synthetic panics: The symbolic politics of designer drugs. In *Synthetic panics*. New York University Press.

Johnston, L. D., Miech, R. A., O'Malley, P. M., Bachman, J. G., Schulenberg, J. E., & Patrick, M. E. (2018). *Monitoring the future national survey results on drug use, 1975–2017: Overview, key findings on adolescent drug use*. Institute for Social Research. https://eric.ed.gov/?id=ED589762

Kanayama, G., Cohane, G. H., & Pope, H. G. (2003). Past anabolic-androgenic steroid use among men admitted for substance abuse treatment: An underrecognized problem? *The Journal of Clinical Psychiatry*, *64*(2), 13902. https://doi.org/10.4088/jcp.v64n0208

Kandel, D. (1975). Stages in adolescent involvement in drug use. *Science*, *190*(4217), 912–914. https://doi.org/10.1126/science.1188374

Kandel, D. B., Kessler, R. C., & Margulies, R. Z. (1978). Antecedents of adolescent initiation into stages of drug use: A developmental analysis. *Journal of Youth and Adolescence*, *7*(1), 13–40. https://doi.org/10.1007/BF01538684

Kim, S., & Selya, A. S. (2020). The relationship between electronic cigarette use and conventional cigarette smoking is largely attributable to shared risk factors. *Nicotine & Tobacco Research*, *22*(7), 1123–1130. https://doi.org/10.1093/ntr/ntz157

Lane, D. C., & DeCamp, W. (2017). "Sports will keep 'em out of trouble": A comparative analysis of substance use among adolescents and young adults. *Journal of Sport and Health Research*, *9*(1), 41–52.

Lemoncelli, J. (2021, May 28). How Lamar Odom conquered his cocaine and sex "demon." *New York Post*. https://nypost.com/2021/05/28/how-lamar-odom-conquered-his-cocaine-and-sex-demon/

Lopez de Subijana, C., Galatti, L., Moreno, R., & Chamorro, J. L. (2020). Analysis of the athletic career and retirement depending on the type of sport: A comparison between individual and team sports. *International Journal of Environmental Research and Public Health*, *17*(24), 9265. https://doi.org/10.3390/ijerph17249265

Macur, J. (2012, October 10). Details of doping scheme paint Armstrong as leader. *The New York Times*. https://www.nytimes.com/2012/10/11/sports/cycling/agency-details-doping-case-against-lance-armstrong.html

Mastroleo, N. R., Marzell, M., Turrisi, R., & Borsari, B. (2012). Do coaches make a difference off the field? The examination of athletic coach influence on early college student drinking. *Addiction Research & Theory*, *20*(1), 64–71. https://doi.org/10.3109/16066359.2011.562621

Mayo Clinic. (n.d.). *Chronic traumatic encephalopathy—Symptoms and causes*. https://www.mayoclinic.org/diseases

-conditions/chronic-traumatic-encephalopathy/symptoms-causes/syc-20370921

McDuff, D. R., & Baron, D. (2005). Substance use in athletics: A sports psychiatry perspective. *Clinics in Sports Medicine*, *24*(4), 885–897. https://doi.org/10.1016/j.csm.2005.06.004

McDuff, D., Stull, T., Castaldelli-Maia, J. M., Hitchcock, M. E., Hainline, B., & Reardon, C. L. (2019). Recreational and ergogenic substance use and substance use disorders in elite athletes: A narrative review. *British Journal of Sports Medicine*, *53*(12), 754–760. https://doi.org/10.1136/bjsports-2019-100669

Mendelsohn, C. P., & Hall, W. (2020). Does the gateway theory justify a ban on nicotine vaping in Australia? *International Journal of Drug Policy*, *78*, 102712. https://doi.org/10.1016/j.drugpo.2020.102712

Merton, R. K. (1938). Social structure and anomie. *American Sociological Review*, *3*(5), 672–682. https://doi.org/10.2307/2084686

National Collegiate Athletic Association. (2018). *NCAA national study on substance use habits of college student-athletes.*

Newsham, G. (September 18, 2021). Why more professional athletes use and rely on cannabis. *New York Post*. https://nypost.com/2021/09/18/why-more-professional-athletes-use-and-rely-on-cannabis/

Nicholson, T. (n.d.). *The IPC decision on the membership status of the Russian Paralympic committee*. International Paralympic Committee. https://www.paralympic.org/news/ipc-decision-membership-status-russian-paralympic-committee

Ohl, F., Fincoeur, B., Lentillon-Kaestner, V., Defrance, J., & Brissonneau, C. (2015). The socialization of young cyclists and the culture of doping. *International Review for the Sociology of Sport*, *50*(7), 865–882. https://doi.org/10.1177/1012690213495534

Outlaw, K. R., Carpenter-Aeby, T., East Carolina University, 201 Rivers, ECU, Greenville, NC 27858, USA, Aeby, V. G., & East Carolina University, 201 Rivers, ECU, Greenville, NC

27858, USA. (2018). Opioids and Athletes: A Growing Problem and a Deadly Combination. *Sports and Exercise Medicine - Open Journal, 4*(3), 63–65. https://doi.org/10.17140/SEMOJ-4-163

Pappa, E., & Kennedy, E. (2013). "It was my thought…he made it a reality": Normalization and responsibility in athletes' accounts of performance-enhancing drug use. *International Review for the Sociology of Sport, 48*(3), 277–294. https://doi.org/10.1177/1012690212442116

Parker, H., Williams, L., & Aldridge, J. (2002). The normalization of "sensible" recreational drug use: Further evidence from the North West England longitudinal study. *Sociology, 36*(4), 941–964. https://doi.org/10.1177/003803850203600408

Parrett, M. (2010). Does steroid use gateway into Marijuana use? Evidence from 2001–2007 monitoring the future data. *Southern Business & Economic Journal, 33*(2), 93–106. https://web.p.ebscohost.com/abstract?direct=true&profile=ehost&scope=site&authtype=crawler&jrnl=0743779X&AN=78096138&h=LBpoobW7my2ooPPbQFCKRDjwzOoVOzeOxmxFHbTcgZ7KKzkzr6GJyRh6O%2bkVkBvJ2w48PEHDlf79A4BflQezhA%3d%3d&crl=c&resultNs=AdminWebAuth&resultLocal=ErrCrlNotAuth&crlhashurl=login.aspx%3fdirect%3dtrue%26profile%3dehost%26scope%3dsite%26authtype%3dcrawler%26jrnl%3d0743779X%26AN%3d78096138

Pate, R. R., Trost, S. G., Levin, S., & Dowda, M. (2000). Sports participation and health-related behaviors among U.S. youth. *Archives of Pediatrics & Adolescent Medicine, 154*(9), 904. https://doi.org/10.1001/archpedi.154.9.904

Perry, B. L., & Pescosolido, B. A. (2012). Social network dynamics and biographical disruption: The case of "first-timers" with mental illness. *American Journal of Sociology, 118*(1), 134–175. https://doi.org/10.1086/666377

Pescosolido, B. A. (1992). Beyond rational choice: The social dynamics of how people seek help. *American Journal of Sociology, 97*(4), 1096–1138.

Reid, M. (2020). A qualitative review of cannabis stigmas at the twilight of prohibition. *Journal of Cannabis Research*, *2*(1), 46. https://doi.org/10.1186/s42238-020-00056-8

Rhodes, T. (2002). The "risk environment": A framework for understanding and reducing drug-related harm. *International Journal of Drug Policy*, *13*(2), 85–94. https://doi.org/10.1016/S0955-3959(02)00007-5

Rhodes, T. (2009). Risk environments and drug harms: A social science for harm reduction approach. *International Journal of Drug Policy*, *20*(3), 193–201. https://doi.org/10.1016/j.drugpo.2008.10.003

Salinas, M., Floodgate, W., & Ralphs, R. (2019). Polydrug use and polydrug markets amongst image and performance enhancing drug users: Implications for harm reduction interventions and drug policy. *International Journal of Drug Policy*, *67*, 43–51. https://doi.org/10.1016/j.drugpo.2019.01.019

Skarberg, K., Nyberg, F., & Engstrom, I. (2009). Multisubstance use as a feature of addiction to anabolic-androgenic steroids. *European Addiction Research*, *15*(2), 99–106. https://doi.org/10.1159/000199045

Striegel, H., Simon, P., Frisch, S., Roecker, K., Dietz, K., Dickhuth, H.-H., & Ulrich, R. (2006). Anabolic ergogenic substance users in fitness-sports: A distinct group supported by the health care system. *Drug and Alcohol Dependence*, *81*(1), 11–19. https://doi.org/10.1016/j.drugalcdep.2005.05.013

Sutherland, E. (1947). Differential association. *Journal of Psychiatry*, *102*, 674–682.

Sznitman, S. R., & Taubman, D. S. (2016). Drug use normalization: A systematic and critical mixed-methods review. *Journal of Studies on Alcohol and Drugs*, *77*(5), 700–709. https://doi.org/10.15288/jsad.2016.77.700

Tamminen, K., & Holt, N. (2012). Adolescent athletes' learning about coping and the roles of parents and coaches. *Psychology of Sport and Exercise*, *13*(1), 69–79. https://doi.org/10.1016/j.psychsport.2011.07.006

Taree, A., Charen, D., Huang, H.-H., Poeran, J., & Colvin, A. (2022). Analysis of surgery rates among 25 national collegiate athletic association sports. *The Physician and Sportsmedicine*, *50*(1), 30–37. https://doi.org/10.1080/00913847.2020.1862632

Turrisi, R., Larimer, M. E., Mallett, K. A., Kilmer, J. R., Ray, A. E., Mastroleo, N. R., Geisner, I. M., Grossbard, J., Tollison, S., Lostutter, T. W., & Montoya, H. (2009). A randomized clinical trial evaluating a combined Alcohol intervention for high-risk college students. *Journal of Studies on Alcohol and Drugs*, *70*(4), 555–567. https://doi.org/10.15288/jsad.2009.70.555

van de Ven, K., & Mulrooney, K. J. D. (2017). Social suppliers: Exploring the cultural contours of the performance and image enhancing drug (PIED) market among bodybuilders in the Netherlands and Belgium. *International Journal of Drug Policy*, *40*, 6–15. https://doi.org/10.1016/j.drugpo.2016.07.009

Waldorf, D., Reinarman, C., & Murphy, S. B. (1991). *Cocaine changes*. Temple University Press.

Walters, P., Hillier, B., Passetti, F., Soni, A., & Treasaden, I. (2021). Diagnosis and management of substance use disorders in athletes. *Advances in Psychiatry and Behavioral Health*, *1*, 135–143. https://doi.org/10.1016/j.ypsc.2021.06.001

Wechsler, H., Davenport, A. E., Dowdall, G. W., Grossman, S. J., & Zanakos, S. I. (1997). Binge drinking, tobacco, and illicit drug use and involvement in college athletics: A survey of students at 140 American colleges. *Journal of American College Health*, *45*(5), 195. https://doi.org/10.1080/07448481.1997.9936884

Weisholtz, D. (Director). (2021, July 2). "I am human": Sha'Carri Richardson speaks out about failing drug test ahead of Tokyo Olympics. NBC Chicago—NBC Today. https://www.nbcchicago.com/news/sports/shacarri-richardson-speaks-out-about-failing-drug-test-ahead-of-tokyo-olympics/2546141/

Winick, C. (1962). Maturing Out of Narcotic Addiction. *Bulletin on Narcotics, 14*(1), 1–7.

Wylleman, P., Reints, A., & Knop, P. D. (2012). A developmental and holistic perspective on athletic career development. In *Managing high performance sport*. Routledge.

Xia, Y., Seaman, S., Hickman, M., Macleod, J., Robertson, R., Copeland, L., McKenzie, J., & De Angelis, D. (2015). Factors affecting repeated cessations of injecting drug use and relapses during the entire injecting career among the Edinburgh addiction cohort. *Drug and Alcohol Dependence, 151*, 76–83. https://doi.org/10.1016/j.drugalcdep.2015.03.005

Yamaguchi, R., Johnston, L. D., & O'Malley, P. (2003). Relationship between student illicit drug use and school drug-testing policies. *Journal of School Health, 73*(4), 159–164. https://doi.org/10.1111/j.1746-1561.2003.tb03596.x

Yusko, D. A., Buckman, J. F., White, H. R., & Pandina, R. J. (2008). Alcohol, Tobacco, illicit drugs, and performance enhancers: A comparison of use by college student athletes and nonathletes. *Journal of American College Health, 57*(3), 281–290. https://doi.org/10.3200/JACH.57.3.281-290

Zhou, J., Heim, D., & Levy, A. (2016). Sports participation and Alcohol use: Associations with sports-related identities and well-being. *Journal of Studies on Alcohol and Drugs, 77*(1), 170–179. https://doi.org/10.15288/jsad.2016.77.170

CHAPTER 4

Alcohol Use and Sport

Without a doubt, alcohol is the most popular controlled psychoactive substance globally, with more than half of individuals aged 15 and over reporting lifetime alcohol consumption and 43% identifying as current (past-year) drinkers (World Health Organization [WHO], 2018). (For reference, less than 20% of the global population used tobacco or nicotine in the past 12 months—and only 2.5% consumed cannabis over this same period.) In nearly every region of the world, the prevalence of past-year drinking peaks among 20- to 24-year-olds, and universally, heavy drinking is most common within this age group. Given the overarching popularity of alcohol, and its concentrated use among young adults, its widespread consumption among athletes should come as no surprise. As we have seen repeatedly throughout this text, athletes often mirror the substance use trends that prevail within their larger societies, with consumption shaped by shared norms, laws, and distribution systems. However, previous chapters have also revealed elevated levels of not only drinking but also problem drinking, within specific sports environments, an apparently paradoxical reality given the well-documented behavioral and physiological toxicity that is associated with certain patterns of alcohol use. In other words, some aspects of the sport risk environment may make some athletes more vulnerable to harmful patterns of alcohol consumption. According to the WHO

(2018), alcohol is the "leading risk factor for premature mortality and morbidity among individuals between 15 and 49 years of age," while the drug accounts for the largest share of deaths among those 15 to 39 (WHO, n.d.). Alcohol use is associated with multiple symptoms of acute cognitive impairment, while overconsumption may lead to dehydration, fatigue, and "hangovers" in the short term (and weight gain and reduced injury recovery in the long term)—side effects that are clearly detrimental to athletic performance (McDuff et al., 2019; WHO, 2018). Emergency department research has additionally identified alcohol consumption as a specific risk for acute sports injury (Gmel et al., 2009). In light of such negative outcomes, how can (some) athletes' enthusiasm for alcohol be explained?

In order to understand this phenomenon, we must keep in mind that the social definition of a drug and its effects may be as important as its scientific pharmacology. If counterintuitive to contemporary observers, alcohol was once regarded not only as an effective medicine, but also as a drug that enhances performance. As documented by sports historian Paul Dimeo (2007, p. 9), among others, alcohol was "considered to be a stimulant and was regularly consumed by competitors"; in fact, the first U.S. man to win the Olympic marathon event in 1904 saw his success attributed to a race course regime of brandy and strychnine (Dimeo, 2007). While alcohol is now recognized as a central nervous system depressant, which slows brain and bodily activity, the drug is also believed to have a "biphasic effect," characterized by neural excitation in the early stages of consumption. Much more recently, the use of alcohol to cure "race day jitters" and bolster confidence in the minutes or hours before competition has been described in multiple studies, even if this practice is not founded within kinesiological evidence (Barnes, 2014; Zhou et al., 2015, 2016).

As few today likely define alcohol as an IPED, it is perhaps more useful to inventory the broader sociological meanings attached to alcohol within different contexts and to further consider how shared social rituals around drinking fit specifically with sport subcultures. Within many regions and societies where alcohol use is prevalent (for example, the Americas, Europe, and the West Pacific), drinking is associated with sociality, celebration, and commiseration, with normative consumption taking place in the company of others. In fact, the primary social "rule" surrounding alcohol may be that one must not drink alone; by contrast, the matters of alcohol type, proper volume, and pattern of consumption may be relegated to mere guidelines, which further vary by venue and demographic. As a drug widely used to form and strengthen social bonds, alcohol may play a significant role within team sports, with participation in drinking events and rituals seen as a sign of individuals' commitment to and identification with a common cause. Moreover, the competition season offers regular opportunities to revel in victory, drown out defeat, or simply seek catharsis after a period of intense training. In the case of professional athletics, alcohol is frequently served to spectators, while major alcohol manufacturers often serve as common sponsors for individual teams or entire leagues (Munro, 2000). Finally, the use, or heavy use, of alcohol may be seen as a hallmark of conventional or hegemonic masculinity within some cultures—and sport remains a social institution that is dominated by male participants.

Of course, in parsing the social logic of alcohol use among athletes, we must continue to be attentive to the dynamics of specific sports risk environments. Alcohol will certainly have different associations with professional women's soccer in Japan, U.S. men's college football, or Olympic swimming and diving. Where this chapter will not focus extensively on the evolution of alcohol laws, policies, and norms within different nations, such relevant aspects of the risk environment will be referenced in order to elucidate patterns of harmful drinking among certain athlete populations or within specific leagues or sports. The relative absence of alcohol research among athletes from regions where alcohol is prohibited or strongly stigmatized probably follows reduced use of this drug in such groups. At the same time, the deep imbrication of drinking within the social habitus of university students in North America, who also represent the largest share of high-performance athletes in the region, is hardly incidental to our questions here.

Defining Patterns of Alcohol Use

Unlike most other controlled substances, alcohol is attended by expert-authored definitions of harmful use; in fact, there are multiple, and sometimes conflicting, measures of problematic drinking patterns, produced by diverse public health, criminal justice, and legislative authorities across the world. It should be pointed out that such standards are made possible by alcohol's status as a "legal," if controlled, substance internationally and within a majority of national regimes; because alcohol manufacturing, labeling, and distribution is subject to regulation, reliable units of consumption can be delineated, and the purity of any individual product can be taken for granted—conditions that do not apply to many other psychoactive substances. At the same time, we may critique the measurement of heavy, binge, and disordered drinking that are offered, as we shall see further on, as artifacts of specific cultural and historical circumstances that further base their recommendations on a physiological norm (e.g., "man of average weight and height") that may align poorly with real-life drinkers (and athletes especially). Moreover, if we are to abide by the tenets of risk environment theory, alcohol- and all drug-related harms are contingent on context, with different aspects of the physical, social, economic, and legal environment encouraging more or less safe drinking habits. Indeed, the contextual nature of harmful drinking is conceded within statutes on drunk or "drink driving," which recognize that gross motor impairment may precede an individual's subjective intoxication; where laws exist, the permitted blood concentration of alcohol (BAC) for driving is often below the levels that would typically result from binge drinking.

While we will review here drinking guidelines from the WHO and select nations with high alcohol prevalence, it should again be noted that different standards reign within different contexts. Indeed, among the 104 countries that have formulated national policies on alcohol, there is no consensus on the definition of an alcoholic beverage or on the volume of a standard alcoholic drink. Less than half classify drinks with at least 0.5% alcohol-by-volume as "alcoholic," while some countries except beer and spirit coolers from this designation (WHO, 2018). Roughly one quarter of countries posit 10 g of alcohol to constitute a "standard drink," yet this definition ranges from 1 to 20 g. Using its own definition for a standard alcoholic drink (12 g of pure alcohol), the WHO identifies "binge" or "heavy episodic" drinking as the consumption of "60 grams or more of pure alcohol on one occasion"—approximately five "standard" drinks in one sitting (although "occasion" remains ambiguous). The same total volume of alcohol is cited in the UK Chief Medical Officer's definition of binge drinking; however, with a "standard drink" listed as 10 mL of alcohol, UK guidance advises against the consumption of more than six drinks in one episode (Drinkaware UK, n.d.). To complicate matters even further, three definitions of binge drinking exist among top federal health and medical authorities in the United States, with metrics varying by age and sex. The Substance Abuse and Mental Health Service Administration (SAMHSA) characterizes binge drinking as "having 5 or more drinks in a row" in its annual study of middle and high school students, while its flagship survey of individuals 12 years and older (the National Survey of Drug Use and Health) defines this practice as the consumption of "5 or more alcoholic drinks for males or 4 or more alcoholic drinks for females on the same occasion" (Johnston et al., 2018; U.S. Department of Health and Human Services, Substance Abuse and Mental Health Services Administration, Center for Behavioral Health Statistics and Quality, 2019). The most precise, if somewhat impractical, advice comes from the National Institute on Alcohol Abuse and Alcoholism (NIAAA), which describes binge drinking in terms of its clinical results—a BAC of 0.08 g/decaliter—noting that this level is typically achieved faster for women, compared to men, within the same time frame (NIAAA, 2022).

The intake of large volumes of alcohol over a less condensed period is a practice often labeled "heavy drinking"; as with binging, definitions vary both between and within national contexts. (Moreover, the WHO does not explicitly address this pattern of alcohol consumption.) The UK's "Low Risk Drinking Guidelines" caution men and women alike to drink no more than 14 "units" of alcohol each week, while spreading consumption over at least three days; the Santé Publique France, by contrast, recommends a weekly ceiling of 10 drinks, for all adults (Drinkaware UK, n.d.; Trimble, 2019). In the United States, SAMHSA (2018) describes heavy drinking as a recurrent pattern of binge drinking, or the consumption of five-plus drinks on five-plus days in the past month. Maintaining its differentiated standards by sex, the NIAAA (2022) stipulates starkly different limits for men and women; men who consume more than 13 drinks per week exceed the healthy threshold, while women pass this marker after only seven. Heavy drinking is still distinct from the diagnosis of alcohol use disorder (AUD), whose symptoms reference a perceived loss of control, negative emotions, and craving. Although heavy and binge drinking are considered risk factors for AUD, they are neither prerequisites nor pathological in themselves (NIAAA, 2022).

Table 1: Definitions of Drinking Behaviors, by Country

	Standard Drink	**Binge/Heavy Episodic Drinking**	**Heavy Drinking**
World Health Organization	12 g of pure alcohol	60+ g alcohol on "one occasion"	Not defined
UK Chief Medical Officer	10 g of pure alcohol	5+ standard drinks (50+ g alcohol) in "one sitting"	14+ "units of alcohol" in 1 week
Santé Publique France	10 g of pure alcohol	6+ drinks in <2 hours (females); 7+ drinks in <2 hours (males)	10+ drinks each week
U.S.—SAMHSA	14 g of pure alcohol	5+ "drinks in a row" OR 4+ drinks on "one occasion" (females); 5+ drinks on "one occasion" (men)	5+ drinks on 5+ days in 1 month
U.S.—NIAAA	14 g of pure alcohol	Achievement of a BAC >0.08	14+ drinks per week (males); 7+ drinks per week (females)

What do we make of these (sometimes vastly) disparate definitions and guidelines? Aside from confirming how culturally situated alcohol consumption is, what do they reveal in terms of the objective consequences of different drinking patterns? As is likely apparent, the definition, and problematization, of binge and heavy drinking relates to the acute and chronic side effects that may follow the intake of significant quantities of alcohol. Whether characterized by four, five, or six drinks, binge drinking might be described as a practice often resulting in significant intoxication, whether intended or unintended. In turn, binge drinking is associated with accidental injury, physical and sexual violence, and poor decision-making, in general—outcomes that warrant attention to the epidemiology and prevention of heavy, rapid alcohol consumption (WHO, 2018). Warnings around heavy drinking, on the other hand, are grounded in evidence concerning the long-term physiological toxicity of alcohol and its manifestation through liver and heart disease, stomach bleeding, as well as multiple cancers (Baan et al., 2007). As noted previously, young adults, college students, and certain athletes report elevated levels of both heavy and binge drinking, compared with other age demographics, nonstudents, and nonathletes. Where Chapter 2 briefly touched on overall levels of alcohol consumption in sport, we will here focus on the prevalence of these potentially risky drinking patterns among athletes, as well as their theoretical explanation. Based on the immediate discussion, it should be apparent that different studies will apply different metrics for binge and heavy drinking, and all rely on retroactive self-reports by athlete participants—an important limitation, given both the issue of social desirability and the demonstrated impact of alcohol on memory. The variability in the preceding definitions might warn us against assuming the inevitable harmfulness of any one athlete's, team's, or sport's drinking patterns, while also illuminating the behavioral and physical concerns that underlie all attempts at measurement.

Epidemiology of Binge and Heavy Drinking in Sport

While estimates of binge drinking differ by competition level, venue, sport, and sex, prior research converges on one important conclusion: a diverse population of athletes reports high levels of heavy, episodic alcohol consumption. A source of much data previously cited here, the National Collegiate Athletic Association's (NCAA) (2018) most recent athlete survey shows that 42% of athletes engaged in binge drinking during the past year, or 44% of male and 39% of female athletes; yet far higher numbers were captured among participants in lacrosse (69% of male, 57% of females), hockey (64%, 56%), and swimming (55%, 49%). Of course, in order to make sense of these numbers, it is necessary to compare them to the prevalence of binge drinking among similar populations. Admittedly, this is a fraught venture. National surveys of young adults in the United States (such as Monitoring the Future, and the National Survey on Drug Use and Health) capture binge drinking in the past month, a measure that yields lower figures but not necessarily comparable ones (Johnston et al., 2018; U.S. Department of Health and Human Services, Substance Abuse and Mental Health Services Administration, Center for Behavioral Health Statistics and Quality, 2019). (For example, in 2018, 34.9% of 18 to 25-year-olds in the United States reported binge alcohol use in the past month.) The yearly prevalence of heavy episodic drinking is reported in the WHO's 2018 Global Status Report on Alcohol, among individuals aged 15 to 19 and 20 to 24; both figures are significantly lower than that captured by the NCAA (42%), at

13.6% and 21.8%, respectively. The same publication includes an estimate for U.S.-based 15- to 19-year-olds specifically—an age group that imperfectly maps to college-aged individuals, which, overall, appears much lower, at 28%. However, disaggregated by sex, these figures point to the need to critically consider the sports risk environment for females, in particular; while 43.9% of males within this category participated in binge drinking in 2016, only 11.2% of females affirm this behavior. Several studies have attempted a direct comparison of binge drinking levels among college-enrolled athletes and nonathletes; however, the age of such research must be conceded, with all such studies reporting on data collected more than 20 years in the past. Nevertheless, several studies suggest that intercollegiate sports participation represents a significant risk factor for binge drinking in college, recording margins of 9% to 19% in favor of student-athletes (Leichliter et al., 1998; Lisha & Sussman, 2010; Martens, Dams-O'Connor, & Beck, 2006; Wechsler et al., 1997).

What about athletes who compete outside of higher education, a context that is already known to foster high rates of risky drinking? Here, the literature is much more scant, limited to a handful of sports, albeit in a wider range of countries. Assessing the prevalence of "alcohol misuse" among a sample of National Rugby League players in Australia, Du Preez et al. (2017) concluded that roughly two-thirds of participants (68.6% preseason and 62.8% in season) met criteria for the diagnosis of hazardous drinking, a designation that reflects the frequency of binge drinking among other practices. Although distressing, this study appears to represent a high-water mark for harmful alcohol use among high-performance athletes outside of college. A 2019 meta-analysis comprising twenty-two studies of current and former elite (professional and Olympic) athletes revealed a modal prevalence of "alcohol misuse" symptoms at 19% of enrolled athletes. Athlete populations exhibiting higher rates of alcohol misuse included South African cricket players, members of the French and Swedish national sports teams, professional or national team soccer players, and elite Gaelic male athletes (Gouttebarge et al., 2019).

While the next section will attempt to apply relevant theoretical frameworks toward the explanation of harmful drinking patterns among athletes, we might first quickly assess any trends emerging from the epidemiological literature. First, the balance of studies among professional/national team athletes reveal high levels of heavy drinking (or "alcohol misuse") among male athletes specifically; moreover, the studies that captured both men's and women's sports report significantly lower rates of harmful alcohol use among females—a finding that echoes the sex disparity in binge drinking among U.S. student-athletes (NCAA, 2018; Schaal et al., 2011). Thus, we might consider the impact of gender, and, specifically, traditional masculinity, within the sports risk environment for alcohol consumption. Next, it may strike the reader that all of the aforementioned studies derive from countries or regions where not only is alcohol use culturally normative but also the overall prevalence of drinking, and binge drinking, is also elevated relative to global averages. Australia, France, Ireland, Sweden, and the United States all report levels of current and heavy episodic drinking that significantly exceed 43% and 18.2%, respectively (a statement that also applies to the European and Americas regions) (WHO, 2018). In light of this data, we might tentatively conclude that the impact of sports participation on alcohol use is at least partially moderated by national drinking culture. A final observation relates to the specific sports highlighted previously, including lacrosse, hockey, swimming, rugby, football (soccer), and cricket. With the exception of swimming, all of these sports are played in teams, an organizational factor that has been identified as amplifying the risk of unhealthy behaviors among athletes (Grunseit et al., 2012). This insight might focus our subsequent inquiries on the interpersonal dynamics of athletic teams, processes of socialization and bonding, and the influence of athlete identity on drinking.

Theorizing the "Alcohol-Sport Nexus" Through Ethic of Sport

Much has been written about how the culture of sport may relate to alarming levels of, or practices related to, alcohol consumption among athletes; indeed many commentators have identified heavy/ drinking as a defining practice within sport subculture. How can a behavior associated with physical impairment fit within a lifestyle or social group oriented around physical excellence? Key norms that have been identified with the culture of sport are instructive in unraveling this paradox, as this unique value system seeks to shape behaviors beyond training and competition. Briefly reviewed in the previous chapter, the ethic of sport is expressed in four major imperatives addressed to "real" athletes (Hughes & Coakley, 1991). First, athletes must prioritize their sports career above everything else, even if it means sacrificing other social, professional, or educational pursuits; it follows that one's primary social obligations are to teammates and coaches. Second, to be an athlete is to constantly pursue improvement, and distinction, in the forms of winning or record-breaking. Striving for better, and aiming toward supremacy, is an essential moral imperative embraced by the true athlete. A third, related, rule is that athletes never back down from a challenge, give in to fear, or relent in the face of pain or possible injury. In fact, sports commitment is demonstrated by running into the proverbial fire and accepting the risk of personal harm. Lastly, to be successful in sport, one must recognize no limits, whether physical or social. Considered in tandem with the previous mandates, this implies that athletes must do whatever it takes to achieve their dream of sports dominance.

More an abstract slate of values than a precise code of conduct, the ethic of sport (as characterized by research) does not posit specific rules or recommendations around alcohol use; by contrast, it might be logically supposed that many sports teams, whether school-based or professional, have explicit policies forbidding alcohol consumption, at least at certain places or times. However, in the interstices of the ethic, it is easy to see how it might encourage heavy drinking, particularly within a group setting. According to the preceding criteria, real athletes not only embrace but also enjoy risk. A practice, such as binge drinking, which is often represented as objectively harmful, may be appealing for this same reason—the consumption of alcohol at dangerous levels may serve as a test of one's courage. Heavy drinking may additionally be framed as an extreme behavior through which an athlete might demonstrate their physiological superiority (or at least their belief in said superiority). In this way, individuals may not binge for the purpose of becoming intoxicated but rather, to prove that they will not, being immune to the effects of alcohol. Of course, given its emphasis on in-group allegiance, the ethic of sport only requires proof of adherence to others in the same social category, and, specifically, one's teammates. This may explain the concentration of heavy drinking within team sports, as well as hazing rituals that demand that initiates imbibe harmful amounts of alcohol—a topic explored below.

How has research demonstrated athletes' adoption of the ethic of sport and its relationship to alcohol consumption? Reflecting on a review of studies that reveal a higher frequency of binge drinking among student-athletes, Lisha and Sussman (2010) consider how such practices might be indicative of athletes' "competitive nature," a characteristic that is further amplified by the sports subculture. Weaver et al. (2013) also showed significant correlations between college athletes' score on indices measuring competitiveness, win orientation, and goal orientation with their self-reported levels of alcohol use. Multiple scholars have documented the psychological strain experienced by student-athletes who are attempting to commit fully to their athletic endeavors, while still keeping their heads above water academically. Heavy alcohol use may function as a coping mechanism for such individuals, caught between the ethic of sport and the demands of school, who embrace the maxim of "work hard, play hard" to justify a potentially damaging behavior (Weaver, 2013). In a survey of over 50,000 U.S. college students, Leichliter et al. (1998) showed that athletes reported higher volumes of alcohol consumption, higher rates of binge drinking—and more negative consequences; student sport leaders, who were more invested in modeling an ideal athlete identity, were additionally shown to drink more than their peers without leadership roles. Putting aside competing priorities, the ethic of sport and its draconian performance mandates have been shown to induce anxiety in not only high performance but also less elite student-athlete populations. In turn, alcohol use may emerge as a situationally convenient means of dealing with the physical, social, and emotional pressures associated with sports involvement (Lisha & Sussman, 2010; Marcello et al., 1989; Martens, Dams-O'Connor, & Beck., 2006; Tricker et al., 1989).

Other commentators have observed how the ethic of sport reflects typically masculine ideals around physical dominance, stoicism, and risk-taking (Berg et al., 2014). Such ideals are not specific to the male-dominated institution of sport, nor are elevated levels of drinking restricted to male athletes. In other words, the heavy alcohol consumption observed among certain populations may speak as much to gender structure as to sports culture (although it is admittedly difficult to disentangle the former from the latter.) The specific impact of traditional masculinity on extreme drinking practices has been captured by studies of hazing rituals among college sports teams. This research shows that not only do a majority of athletes experience hazing at the point of team initiation but also that over half experience alcohol-related hazing (e.g., drinking contests) (Hoover, 1999). The balance of extant research suggests that male athletes are more likely to experience hazing (of all varieties) than their female counterparts, a finding that resonates with the gender disparity in alcohol consumption presented previously (Allan et al., 2019; Hoover, 1999; Kerschner & Allan, 2021; Lafferty et al., 2017). At the same time, studies show that female athletes are hardly immune to hazing practices, alcohol-involved or otherwise, data that may point to the institutionalization of hegemonic masculinity in sport (Hamilton, 2013; Waldron, 2015). Indeed, a 2013 study of initiation rituals among Canadian college athletes concluded that females were more likely to be hazed within collision sports that were historically male-dominated (Hamilton, 2013). Finally, it is possible that athletic participation, and the ethic of sport, may be refracted differently across the gender binary, with male athletes more vulnerable to the adoption of "toxic jock" identities, a status that is largely unrelated to degree of sports involvement. In studies of high school athletes, Miller et al. determined that male "jocks" reported a higher frequency of binge drinking, nonfamily violence, and delinquency (Miller et al., 2003, 2006, 2007). While "jock identity" has been measured as an almost independent, subjective social status, the next section will consider how individuals' strength of "athlete" identification may also predict alcohol consumption patterns.

Where the culture of sport may promote norms and values supportive of heavy drinking, it is also important to consider how the broader risk environment—within and beyond athletics—may moderate the effects of this ethic. Studies just cited suggest that other aspects of the social sphere may neutralize, or exacerbate, messaging that promotes risky, competitive, or otherwise extreme behaviors as a means of proving oneself a "real" athlete; female athletes, as well as individuals who participate in nonteam or noncontact sports, are less likely to perform the ethic's dicta through binge or heavy drinking. Research conducted among athletes and nonathletes alike has additionally highlighted the salience of the economic risk environment. Across the world, individuals from lower-income countries—and lower-income backgrounds—are less likely to consume alcohol, a finding that has been reproduced among college student-athletes (NCAA, 2018; WHO, 2018). (It may also be worth wondering how the association between athletics and alcohol might be shaped by socioeconomic status; recent surveys have found that that children from lower- and middle-income backgrounds are less likely to become involved with sports (Riser-Kositsky & Peele, 2021).) As noted earlier, alcohol is frequently embedded in the physical culture of sports competition at the university and professional levels. Athletes who compete in arenas where alcohol is sold, consumed, and advertised on site may be more likely to celebrate their victories by drinking (Grunseit et al., 2012; Williams et al., 2006). Lastly, league or institutional policies sanctioning certain kinds of substance use may indirectly encourage the consumption of alcohol over other drugs, whose presence is explicitly proscribed or captured by drug testing (O'Brien & Lyons, 2000).

Drinking to Fit in: Socialization Theories of Alcohol Use Among Student-Athletes

Research on patterns of alcohol use among college student-athletes has zeroed in on a primal motivation underlying individuals' escalating alcohol consumption: the desire to fit in. In order to gauge peer influence on individuals' emerging alcohol behaviors, studies have deployed two fundamental metrics: team norms, or unofficial rules, around alcohol use (as perceived by a team member her/himself) and strength of athlete identity, a measure used to estimate the salience of team norms for any one individual's attitudes and actions. While drawing on fundamental theories that span criminology, sociology, and psychology (such as differential association and selective socialization, discussed in Chapter 3), research in this vein offers the advantage of identifying multiple targets for harm reduction, interventions that will be presented in the final section of this chapter.

Turning first to perceived norms of alcohol (and other drug) use among student-athletes, it should be noted that such "rules" are captured in different ways, allowing researchers to not only triangulate their data but also capture surprising disjunctures between opinions and behaviors. In other words, in attempting to mold our behavior to the specifications of valued others, we typically consider what our models both think and do, a binary that maps roughly to what theorists call injunctive norms and descriptive norms. Injunctive norms comprise our perceptions of peer approval, or disapproval, for different behaviors— moral estimations that we might consider before engaging in a possibly unacceptable activity. Anticipating tacit condemnation or explicit ostracization by our team, we might constrain our consumption of alcohol, or limit drinking to certain times and places where it will not be observed. In theory, descriptive norms may be based on more empirical evidence, as they refer to our perceptions of what peers actually do (as well as how/often they do it and with what rewards or consequences) (Cialdini & Goldstein, 2004). If we observe our teammates or fellow athletes consistently enjoying a postworkout beer or celebrating a victory by binge drinking, we are more likely to ourselves indulge, having understood this activity to be normal if not pleasurable (Graupensperger et al., 2020). Both injunctive and descriptive group norms have been shown to relate to student-athletes' substance use behaviors, although questions remain about accuracy and directionality. On the one hand, there is evidence to suggest that college students often overestimate their peers' level and frequency of alcohol consumption, a potentially deleterious miscalculation that is nevertheless susceptible to correction (Neighbors et al., 2006). More troublesome is evidence of a reverse correlation between individuals' drinking and perception of descriptive norms. Rather than modeling their consumption on peer behaviors, student-athletes who drink heavily may project their own predilections onto teammates, implicitly rationalizing this behavior as normative.

Longitudinal studies—which track behaviors or other outcomes over time and are thus capable of assessing the directionality of associations—have both confirmed the salience of injunctive and descriptive norms in shaping student-athletes' drinking patterns and illuminated problems of overestimation and projection. Tracking college club athletes' alcohol use frequency over one academic year, Graupensperger et al. (2020) found evidence of all three phenomena. On average, athletes reported having at least one alcoholic drink each week—but guessed that their fellow teammates consumed at least two. At the level of individuals, students who indicated drinking more often also estimated a higher frequency of alcohol use among their peers at any given time point. Moreover, injunctive norm perceptions appeared to influence athletes' drinking over time, meaning that individuals reduced (or increased) the frequency of alcohol use in line with their beliefs around peer approval. Where other studies have shown young adults to be susceptible to the perceived opinions and actions of more general referent groups (e.g., "typical college students," fellow dorm residents, same sex/race/ethnicity peers), sport teams may represent a particularly close-knit collective with higher levels of behavioral influence on their members (Neighbors et al., 2007). Indeed, individuals may be more capable of observing the actions of a small proximal group, while additionally valuing the opinion of people more like themselves, especially if their own membership may be threatened by participation in non-normative behavior.

A host of studies have, in fact, shown that the subjective strength of team/group membership (often conceptualized as "athlete identity") is related to drinking, results that may suggest conformity to in-group alcohol use norms. In a cross-sectional study of university athletes in the UK, Zhou et al. (2016) found that individuals who scored higher on a common measure of athletic identity (the Athletic Identity Measurement Scale [AIMS]) also reported higher levels of alcohol consumption, although this effect was moderated by sports type; specifically, team sport athletes exhibited a positive association between athletic identity and drinking, while individual sport athletes tended to drink less as athletic identity increased. Similarly, Grossbard et al. (2009) established a positive relationship between student-athletes' "attraction to team," perceived alcohol use norms, and level of drinking. Moving toward interventions that may be effective in deterring harmful drinking patterns, it may appear as though "athletic identity" is a difficult variable to modify, if one that should be targeted at all. However, as we will see, it is possible to strengthen other aspects of individuals' sense of self, or diversify their referent groups, in order to reduce the risk of negative alcohol outcomes.

What Works: Evidence-Based Interventions to Reduce Alcohol-Related Risk Among Athletes

In identifying common predictors of heavy alcohol consumption, as well as the sociological mechanisms through which they operate, the research reviewed previously highlights many promising sites of intervention to reduce harmful drinking patterns among athletes: sports-specific subcultural values that encourage risk-taking and extreme physical behaviors; models of masculinity that endorse dangerous forms of competition; a physical environment saturated with alcohol advertisement and sales; overwhelming and unrealistic pressures, combined with inadequate support, for college student-athletes; erroneous perceptions of peer drinking norms, and/or their unquestioned enactment; and personal and social identification with athletics at the expense of other possible roles and affiliations. Obviously, all of these risk-promoting factors are not inherently negative. Sensitivity to peer or team attitudes, a strong sense of athlete identity, and a desire for sports success are hardly pathological attributes. Even if the "ethic of sport" may lead to physical (and social) harms when followed to the extreme, it may also foster a culture of athletic excellence. In practice, this means that efforts to decrease harmful drinking patterns among athletes often seek to moderate the impact of such risk factors, rather than eliminating them altogether. While many programs have been deployed toward this end, this section will showcase those that have been shown to be effective in reducing heavy or binge drinking, and associated alcohol harms, as well as the conditions under which they have succeeded.

Revising the Standard: Norm-Based Interventions

Unsurprisingly, most evidence-based interventions to reduce harmful drinking among athletes have targeted those competing within institutions of higher education. On the one hand, college enrollment represents an indisputable intensifier of alcohol consumption and related risk; on the other, such athletes are both easy to identify and amenable to participation incentives (or requirements). Given the considerable research revealing the salience of referent groups, such as teammates, on individuals' substance use behaviors, the most tested type of drinking intervention among student-athletes leverages—and seeks to correct—their normative perceptions around alcohol. As shown by Graupensperger et al. (2020), among others, college athletes tend to overestimate their peers' level of alcohol consumption, sometimes severely (Dams-O'Connor et al., 2007; Martens, Dams-O'Connor, Duffy-Paiement, et al., 2006). For this reason, several successful interventions have attempted to recalibrate student-athletes' "descriptive norms" by allowing them access to accurate information on team drinking practices. After all, if wildly distorted notions of peer drinking drive individuals to overconsumption, it might be enough to simply set the record straight.

Indeed, social norms interventions within student-athlete populations have been shown to be effective—but only under certain circumstances. Efforts to broadly and passively expose athletes to real statistics on alcohol consumption among their peers (for example, through posters, newspaper ads, mailed materials, and classroom presentations) have shown repeated success in correcting individuals' misperceptions of campus drinking norms; however, the impact of such campaigns on student-athletes' actual drinking levels is more ambiguous (Perkins & Craig, 2006; Thombs & Hamilton, 2002). Where time-limited interventions (that saturate the student environment with relevant messaging over a discrete intervention period) have not proven effective in lowering alcohol consumption, prolonged marketing campaigns that target students over a number of years have reduced numerous types of harmful drinking (Perkins & Craig, 2006; Thombs & Hamilton, 2002). Likewise, a 2010 study of nonelite, community-level football teams in Australia determined that club-level efforts to shift the culture of drinking through responsible alcohol service training and restrictions on drinking games (combined with the competitive repricing of no- or low-alcohol drinking) led to a significant reduction in excessive drinking among club members themselves (Kingsland et al., 2015).

A more consistent method of shifting both perceived norms and resultant behaviors directly leverages peer influence, by immediately disclosing the results of surveys on alcohol use to athlete participants. These feedback interventions cut out the unknown "middle-man"—researchers and educators outside the target population—and instead give real-time information to individual athletes in the company of their teammates. Using live, interactive norms presentations among student-athletes at two universities, Labrie et al. (2009) showed persistent reductions in participant drinking at both 1 month, and 2 months, post intervention. This method, which utilized wireless, handheld keypads that reported respondents' survey answers instantaneously, also confirmed the mediating influence of perceived descriptive norms in shaping college athletes' drinking behaviors. Similar interventions targeting athletes who previously met criteria for binge drinking have shown similar success in reducing harmful alcohol use, while individually delivered normative feedback also holds promise (Cimini et al., 2015; Neighbors et al., 2004).

Norms-based interventions seek to revise faulty knowledge of peer drinking practices, a relatively soft target that athletes may be eager to improve. By contrast, programs that attempt to alter or shift athlete identity face a significantly greater challenge, given the histories and emotions that shape individuals' complex sense of self. Nevertheless, different dimensions of athlete identity may be modulated indirectly, through interventions that recognize that individuals with stronger athlete social identification are more susceptible to following team drinking norms, real or perceived. Where such programs have yet to be tested, a wealth of preliminary research has parsed the relevant elements of athlete identity that heighten alcohol risk. For example, Meca et al. (2021) isolated negative affectivity—or fear and stress related to athletic failure—as a particularly strong predictor of hazardous drinking among college student-athletes. Such a finding may inform interventions that seek to support student-athletes in navigating the "sports-studies" balance, reducing psychological stress and, consequently, the use of alcohol as a coping mechanism. Moreover, research that illuminates a negative relationship between athletic identity and alcohol consumption may have implications for prevention efforts. Zhou et al. (2015) found that among college competitors in individual sports (e.g., tennis, swimming), higher scores on athlete identity indices were associated with lower levels of hazardous alcohol use, a relationship that perhaps reflects knowledge of alcohol's negative impact on athletic performance. While this information might shape educational interventions emphasizing the incompatibility of alcohol use with athletic excellence, data generated from studies of team sports participants is also relevant. Individuals who compete in team sports typically report higher levels of athlete identity and more frequent engagement in harmful drinking (Zhou et al., 2015). Here, the influence of team alcohol norms is again revealed and emerges as a significant site for intervention, particularly in light of studies showing that strong athletic identification increases the risk of normative misperceptions (Grossbard et al., 2009; Martens, Dams-O'Connor, Duffy-Paiement, et al., 2006).

It might further be noted that individuals' strength of athletic identity has recently been correlated with their intentions to seek help for alcohol use, a potentially important finding in light of earlier research showing that student-athletes are less likely to actually seek help for mental health concerns (Moreland et al., 2018; Young, 2021). At the same time, evidence-based interventions specific to the treatment of AUD among athletes are conspicuously few. To date, two programs have been assessed to show positive effects on alcohol use among enrolled athletes: The Optimum Performance Program in Sports (TOPPS), a 12-meeting intervention that engages individuals' athletic goals to motivate reduction of harmful substance use, and the mindfulness–acceptance–commitment model, which has been piloted among female college athletes (Chow et al., 2015; Donohue et al., 2018; Gross et al., 2018). Beyond explicitly addressing participants' identities as athlete in delivering care, these programs also depart from widely discredited "zero tolerance" models of discouraging drug and alcohol use, which fail to deter harmful drinking through negative sanctions. Moreover, while drug testing programs typically exclude alcohol, as a substance that is not usually "banned," emerging evidence suggests that alcohol use may be displaced by the consumption of other substances with less physical and behavioral toxicity, notably, cannabis. Policies that test and sanction athletes for the consumption of substances that represent potentially safer substitutes for alcohol might be considered to exacerbate the risk of drug-related harms, whether physical, psychological, or social (Subbaraman, 2016).

Reflection Points

1. How are risk factors for alcohol misuse shared between college student-athletes and college/university students at large?

2. Why might male student-athletes and contact and club sport participants report higher levels of binge and heavy drinking?

3. How might policies that ban or sanction the use of illicit drugs impact athletes' consumption of alcohol?

Glossary

Athletic Identity: The degree to which an individuals' sense of self, self-worth, and social status is grounded in their participation in athletics. Athletic identity is operationalized and measured in different ways in scholarly research, with common dimensions referencing the supremacy of athletic participation in shaping personal identity, the exclusion of other sites of identity, and the emotion related to athletic success.

Binge Drinking: While definitions of binge or "heavy episodic" drinking are not universal, most stipulate the consumption of multiple (four-plus) alcoholic beverages within a limited time period (e.g., "one occasion"), resulting in subjective intoxication and an objectively elevated level of alcohol in the blood.

Culture or Ethic of Sport: A value system unique to athletes, which emphasizes the prioritization of sports activities and relationships, the relentless pursuit of athletic success, risk-taking or "playing through pain," and the dismissal of physical or other limitations.

Evidence-Based Intervention or Program: A set of problem-oriented activities that has been shown, through scientific research and preferably experimental methods, to effectively achieve its targeted ends—for example, the reduction of potentially harmful drinking patterns.

Heavy Drinking: As with "binge drinking," there exists no global standard for heavy drinking; however, this term generally refers to the consumption of large volumes of alcohol over an extended time period, resulting in chronic physical or mental illness (e.g., liver disease).

REFERENCES

Allan, E. J., Kerschner, D., & Payne, J. M. (2019). College student hazing experiences, attitudes, and perceptions: Implications for prevention. *Journal of Student Affairs Research and Practice*, *56*(1), 32–48. https://doi.org/10.1080/19496591.2018.1490303

Baan, R., Straif, K., Grosse, Y., Secretan, B., El Ghissassi, F., Véronique, B., Andrea, A., & Vincent, C. (2007). Carcinogenicity of alcoholic beverages. *The Lancet Oncology*, *8*(4), 292–293. https://doi.org/10.1016/s1470-2045(07)70099-2

Barnes, M. (2014). Alcohol: Impact on sports performance and recovery in male athletes. *Sports Medicine*, *44*, 909–919.

Berg, E. C., Migliaccio, T. A., & Anzini-Varesio, R. (2014). Female football players, the sport ethic and the masculinity-sport nexus. *Sport in Society*, *17*(2), 176–189. https://doi.org/10.1080/17430437.2013.828699

Chow, G. M., Donohue, B., Pitts, M., Loughran, T., Schubert, K. N., Gavrilova, Y., & Diaz, E. (2015). Results of a single case controlled study of the optimum performance program in sports in a collegiate athlete. *Clinical Case Studies*, *14*(3), 191–209. https://doi.org/10.1177/1534650114548313

Cialdini, R. B., & Goldstein, N. (2004). Social influence: Compliance and conformity. *Annual Review of Psychology*, *55*, 34.

Cimini, M. D., Monserrat, J. M., Sokolowski, K. L., Dewitt-Parker, J. Y., Rivero, E. M., & McElroy, L. A. (2015). Reducing high-risk drinking among student-athletes: The effects of a targeted athlete-specific brief intervention. *Journal of American College Health*, *63*(6), 343–352. https://doi.org/10.1080/07448481.2015.1031236

Dams-O'Connor, K., Martin, J. L., & Martens, M. P. (2007). Social norms and alcohol consumption among intercollegiate athletes: The role of athlete and nonathlete reference groups. *Addictive Behaviors*, *32*(11), 2657–2666. https://doi.org/10.1016/j.addbeh.2007.04.030

Dimeo, P. (2007). *A history of drug use in sport 1876–1976: Beyond good and evil*. Routledge.

Donohue, B., Gavrilova, Y., Galante, M., Gavrilova, E., Loughran, T., Scott, J., Chow, G., Plant, C., & Allen, D. (2018). Controlled evaluation of an optimization approach to mental health and sport performance. *Journal of Clinical Sport Psychology*, *12*, 1–42. https://doi.org/10.1123/jcsp.2017-0054

Drinkaware UK. (n.d.). *UK alcohol unit guidance: CMOs' low risk drinking guidelines*. https://www.drinkaware.co.uk/facts/alcoholic-drinks-and-units/low-risk-drinking-guidelines#singleoccasiondrinking

Du Preez, E. J., Graham, K. S., Gan, T. Y., Moses, B., Ball, C., & Kuah, D. E. (2017). Depression, anxiety, and alcohol use in elite rugby league players over a competitive season.

Clinical Journal of Sport Medicine, 27(6), 530–535. https://doi.org/10.1097/JSM.0000000000000411

Gmel, G., Kuendig, H., & Daeppen, J.-B. (2009). Sport and alcohol: An emergency department study in Switzerland. *European Journal of Sport Science, 9*(1), 11–22. https://doi.org/10.1080/17461390802579111

Gouttebarge, V., Castaldelli-Maia, J. M., Gorczynski, P., Hainline, B., Hitchcock, M. E., Kerkhoffs, G. M., Rice, S. M., & Reardon, C. L. (2019). Occurrence of mental health symptoms and disorders in current and former elite athletes: A systematic review and meta-analysis. *British Journal of Sports Medicine, 53*(11), 700–706. https://doi.org/10.1136/bjsports-2019-100671

Graupensperger, S., Turrisi, R., Jones, D., & Evans, M. B. (2020). Longitudinal associations between perceptions of peer group drinking norms and students' alcohol use frequency within college sport teams. *Alcoholism: Clinical and Experimental Research, 44*(2), 541–552. https://doi.org/10.1111/acer.14270

Gross, M., Moore, Z. E., Gardner, F. L., Wolanin, A. T., Pess, R., & Marks, D. R. (2018). An empirical examination comparing the mindfulness-acceptance-commitment approach and psychological skills training for the mental health and sport performance of female student athletes. *International Journal of Sport and Exercise Psychology, 16*(4), 431–451. https://doi.org/10.1080/1612197X.2016.1250802

Grossbard, J., Hummer, J., LaBrie, J., Pederson, E., & Neighbors, C. (2009). Is substance use a team sport? Attraction to team, perceived norms, and Alcohol and Marijuana use among male and female intercollegiate Athletes. *Journal of Applied Sport Psychology, 21*(3), 247–261. https://doi.org/10.1080/10413200903019145

Grunseit, A. C., MacNiven, R., Orr, R., Grassmayr, M., Kelly, B., Davies, D., Colagiuri, S., & Bauman, A. E. (2012). Australian athletes' health behaviours and perceptions of role modelling and marketing of unhealthy products. *Health Promotion Journal of Australia, 23*(1), 63–69. https://doi.org/10.1071/HE12063

Hamilton, R. (2013). An examination of the Rookie Hazing experiences of university athletes in Canada. *Canadian Journal of Social Research*, *3*(1), 35–48.

Hoover, N. (1999). *National survey: Initiation rites and athletics for NCAA sports teams*. Alfred University.

Hughes, R., & Coakley, J. (1991). Positive deviance among athletes: The implications of overconformity to the sport ethic. *Sociology of Sport Journal*, *8*(4), 307–325. https://doi.org/10.1123/ssj.8.4.307

Johnston, L. D., Miech, R. A., O'Malley, P. M., Bachman, J. G., Schulenberg, J. E., & Patrick, M. E. (2018). *Monitoring the future national survey results on drug use, 1975–2017: Overview, key findings on adolescent drug use*. Institute for Social Research. https://eric.ed.gov/?id=ED589762

Kerschner, D., & Allan, E. (2021). Examining the nature and extent of hazing at five NCAA division III institutions and considering the implications for prevention. *Journal of Amateur Sport*, *7*(1), 95–118. https://doi.org/10.17161/jas.v7i1.13632

Kingsland, M., Wolfenden, L., Tindall, J., Rowland, B. C., Lecathelinais, C., Gillham, K. E., Dodds, P., Sidey, M. N., Rogerson, J. C., McElduff, P., Crundall, I., & Wiggers, J. H. (2015). Tackling risky alcohol consumption in sport: A cluster randomised controlled trial of an alcohol management intervention with community football clubs. *Journal of Epidemiology & Community Health*, *69*(10), 993–999. https://doi.org/10.1136/jech-2014-204984

Labrie, J. W., Hummer, J. F., Huchting, K. K., & Neighbors, C. (2009). A brief live interactive normative group intervention using wireless keypads to reduce drinking and alcohol consequences in college student athletes. *Drug and Alcohol Review*, *28*(1), 40–47. https://doi.org/10.1111/j.1465-3362.2008.00012.x

Lafferty, M. E., Wakefield, C., & Brown, H. (2017). "We do it for the team"—Student-athletes' initiation practices and their impact on group cohesion. *International Journal of Sport and*

Exercise Psychology, *15*(4), 438–446. https://doi.org/10.1080/16 12197X.2015.1121507

Leichliter, J. S., Meilman, P. W., Presley, C. A., & Cashin, J. R. (1998). Alcohol use and related consequences among students with varying levels of involvement in college athletics. *Journal of American College Health*, *46*(6), 257. https://doi.org/10.1080/07448489809596001

Lisha, N. E., & Sussman, S. (2010). Relationship of high school and college sports participation with alcohol, tobacco, and illicit drug use: A review. *Addictive Behaviors*, *35*(5), 399–407. https://doi.org/10.1016/j.addbeh.2009.12.032

Marcello, R. J., Danish, S. J., & Stolberg, A. L. (1989). An evaluation of strategies developed to prevent substance abuse among student-athletes. *The Sport Psychologist*, *3*(3), 196–211.

Martens, M. P., Dams-O'Connor, K., & Beck, N. C. (2006). A systematic review of college student-athlete drinking: Prevalence rates, sport-related factors, and interventions. *Journal of Substance Abuse Treatment*, *31*(3), 305–316. https://doi.org/10.1016/j.jsat.2006.05.004

Martens, M. P., Dams-O'Connor, K., Duffy-Paiement, C., & Gibson, J. T. (2006). Perceived alcohol use among friends and alcohol consumption among college athletes. *Psychology of Addictive Behaviors*, *20*(2), 178–184. https://doi.org/10.1037/0893-164X.20.2.178

McDuff, D., Stull, T., Castaldelli-Maia, J. M., Hitchcock, M. E., Hainline, B., & Reardon, C. L. (2019). Recreational and ergogenic substance use and substance use disorders in elite athletes: A narrative review. *British Journal of Sports Medicine*, *53*(12), 754–760. https://doi.org/10.1136/bjsports-2019-100669

Meca, A., Allison, K., Kubilus, R., Olthuis, J. V., Merrill, J. E., Zamboanga, B. L., Wyrick, D., Milroy, J. J., & Carr, K. (2021). Dimensions of athletic identity and their associations with drinking behaviors among a national sample of university athletes in the United States. *Journal of Youth and Adolescence*, *50*(12), 2363–2373. https://doi.org/10.1007/s10964-021-01503-2

Miller, K. E., Hoffman, J. H., Barnes, G. M., Farrell, M. P., Sabo, D., & Melnick, M. J. (2003). Jocks, gender, race, and adolescent problem drinking. *Journal of Drug Education*, *33*(4), 445–462. https://doi.org/10.2190/XPV5-JD5L-RYLK-UMJA

Miller, K. E., Melnick, M. J., Barnes, G. M., Sabo, D., & Farrell, M. P. (2007). Athletic involvement and adolescent delinquency. *Journal of Youth and Adolescence*, *36*(5), 711–723. https://doi.org/10.1007/s10964-006-9123-9

Miller, K. E., Melnick, M. J., Farrell, M. P., Sabo, D. F., & Barnes, G. M. (2006). Jocks, gender, Binge drinking, and adolescent violence. *Journal of Interpersonal Violence*, *21*(1), 105–120. https://doi.org/10.1177/0886260505281662

Moreland, J. J., Coxe, K. A., & Yang, J. (2018). Collegiate athletes' mental health services utilization: A systematic review of conceptualizations, operationalizations, facilitators, and barriers. *Journal of Sport and Health Science*, *7*(1), 58–69. https://doi.org/10.1016/j.jshs.2017.04.009

Munro, G. (2000). Challenging the culture of sport and alcohol. *International Journal of Drug Policy*, *11*(3), 199–202. https://doi.org/10.1016/S0955-3959(00)00056-6

National Collegiate Athletic Association. (2018). *NCAA National Study on Substance Use Habits of College Student-Athletes*.

National Institute on Alcohol Abuse and Alcoholism. (2022). *Alcohol facts and statistics*. https://www.niaaa.nih.gov/publications/brochures-and-fact-sheets/alcohol-facts-and-statistics

Neighbors, C., Dillard, A., & Lewis, M. (2006). Normative misperceptions and temporal precedence of perceived norms and drinking. *Journal of Studies on Alcohol and Drugs*, *67*(2), 290–299. https://pubmed.ncbi.nlm.nih.gov/16562412/

Neighbors, C., Larimer, M. E., & Lewis, M. A. (2004). Targeting misperceptions of descriptive drinking norms: Efficacy of a computer-delivered personalized normative feedback intervention. *Journal of Consulting and Clinical Psychology*, *72*(3), 434–447. https://doi.org/10.1037/0022-006X.72.3.434

Neighbors, C., Lee, C. M., Lewis, M. A., Fossos, N., & Larimer, M. E. (2007). Are social norms the best predictor of outcomes among heavy-drinking college students? *Journal of Studies on Alcohol and Drugs, 68*(4), 556–565.

O'Brien, C., & Lyons, F. (2000). Alcohol and the athlete. *Sports Medicine, 29*, 295–300. https://doi.org/10.2165/00007256-200029050-00001

Perkins, H. W., & Craig, D. W. (2006). A successful social norms campaign to reduce Alcohol misuse among college student-athletes. *Journal of Studies on Alcohol, 67*(6), 880–889. https://doi.org/10.15288/jsa.2006.67.880

Riser-Kositsky, M., & Peele, H. (2021, July 30). Statistics on school sports: How many students play sports? which sports do they play? *Education Week*. https://www.edweek.org/leadership/statistics-on-school-sports-how-many-students-play-sports-which-sports-do-they-play/2021/07

Schaal, K., Tafflet, M., Nassif, H., Thibault, V., Pichard, C., Alcotte, M., Guillet, T., Helou, N. E., Berthelot, G., Simon, S., & Toussaint, J.-F. (2011). Psychological balance in high level athletes: Gender-based differences and sport-specific patterns. *PLoS ONE, 6*(5), e19007. https://doi.org/10.1371/journal.pone.0019007

Subbaraman, M. S. (2016). Substitution and complementarity of alcohol and cannabis: A review of the literature. *Substance Use & Misuse, 51*(11), 1399–1414. https://doi.org/10.3109/10826084.2016.1170145

Thombs, D. L., & Hamilton, M. J. (2002). Effects of a social norm feedback campaign on the drinking norms and behavior of division I student-athletes. *Journal of Drug Education, 32*(3), 227–244. https://doi.org/10.2190/2UYU-6X9M-RJ65-3YYH

Tricker, R., Cook, D., & McGuire, R. (1989). Issues related to drug abuse in college athletics: Athletes at risk. *The Sport Psychologist, 3*(2), 155–165. https://journals.humankinetics.com/view/journals/tsp/3/2/article-p155.xml

Trimble, M. (2019). *Health officials say French should drink less wine*. U.S. News & World Report. www.usnews.com/news/national-news/articles/2019-03-29/health-officials-say-french-should-drink-less-wine-only-2-glasses-a-day

U.S. Department of Health and Human Services, Substance Abuse and Mental Health Services Administration, Center for Behavioral Health Statistics and Quality. (2019). *National survey on drug use and health, 2018*. Substance Abuse and Mental Health Services Administration. https://datafiles.samhsa.gov/

Waldron, J. (2015). Predictors of mild hazing, severe hazing, and positive initiation rituals in sport. *International Journal of Sports Science & Coaching*, *10*(6), 1089–1101. https://journals.sagepub.com/doi/abs/10.1260/1747-9541.10.6.1089

Weaver, C., Martens, M., & Cadigan, J. (2013). Sport-related achievement motivation and alcohol outcomes: An athlete-specific risk factor among intercollegiate athletes. *Addictive Behaviors*, *38*, 2930–2936. https://doi.org/10.1016/j.addbeh.2013.08.021

Wechsler, H., Davenport, A. E., Dowdall, G. W., Grossman, S. J., & Zanakos, S. I. (1997). Binge drinking, tobacco, and illicit drug use and involvement in college athletics: A survey of students at 140 American colleges. *Journal of American College Health*, *45*(5), 195. https://doi.org/10.1080/07448481.1997.9936884

Williams, R. D., Perko, M., Belcher, D., Leaver-Dunn, D. D., Usdan, S. L., & Leeper, J. D. (2006). Use of social ecology model to address Alcohol use among college athletes. *American Journal of Health Studies*, *21*, 228–237.

World Health Organization. (2018). *Global status report on Alcohol and health 2018*. https://apps.who.int/iris/handle/10665/352428

World Health Organization. (n.d.). *Alcohol*. Health Topics. https://www.who.int/health-topics/alcohol

Young, M. G. (2021). *The role of athletic identity in general mental health and Alcohol-related help-seeking intentions of college students*. https://doi.org/10.25777/JMYT-NQ19

Zhou, J., Heim, D., & Levy, A. (2016). Sports participation and Alcohol use: Associations with sports-related identities and well-being. *Journal of Studies on Alcohol and Drugs*, *77*(1), 170–179. https://doi.org/10.15288/jsad.2016.77.170

Zhou, J., Heim, D., & O'Brien, K. (2015). Alcohol consumption, athlete identity, and happiness among student sportspeople as a function of sport-type. *Alcohol and Alcoholism*, *50*(5), 617–623. https://doi.org/10.1093/alcalc/agv030

CHAPTER 5

Opioid Use and Sport

In the summer of 2015, as the (now widely recognized) North American opioid crisis was beginning to generate national headlines, the popular U.S. weekly *Sports Illustrated* published an investigation whose title proclaimed a startling thesis: "How Painkillers Are Turning Youth Athletes into Heroin Addicts" (Wertheim & Rodriguez, 2015). Apart from using stigmatizing language, the article demanded sympathy and support for school- and college-age athletes who had been exposed to potent opioid medications such as OxyContin through "dangerous and inappropriate prescription practices," subsequently initiating use of illicit opioids, namely heroin. By its own assertion, the magazine's report drew largely on anecdotal evidence depicting a swell in opioid use among young athletes, conceding that "hard data" was "difficult to come by"—a statement that still stands. In the absence of comprehensive statistics, the article builds its story through what Reinarman (1994, p. 159) called the "routinization of caricature—rhetorically recrafting the worst cases into typical cases." The tragic overdose deaths of three high school athletes are recast as harbingers of a hidden epidemic, a narrative supported by a handful of law enforcement and treatment professionals. Nevertheless, the story did succeed in predicting one emergent trend within an international emergency that continues to rage: efforts to restrict medical access to POs (such as oxycodone) have pushed many dependent consumers to purchase pills from illicit markets or transition to categorically illegal opioids like heroin and nonpharmaceutical fentanyl.

While alarm bells surrounding a purported athlete-opioid crisis first sounded in the mid-2010s, such concerns have yet to fade, even as extensive evidence has not materialized. In part, the traction of this scare is linked to a real, multinational overdose surge that continues to intensify and shift, evading effective intervention (CDC Injury Center, 2022b). Drug-related mortality has reached historical peaks in the United States (and Canada)—exceeding 100,000 deaths in 2021—while the age distribution of fatal overdose victims has shifted downward (Government of Canada, 2022; Kaiser Family Foundation [KFF], n.d.). The persistent public connection between opioid use and sport, however, likely derives from a series of high-profile athlete deaths linked to opioid (and other drug) use. For example, the 2019 overdose of Major League Baseball (MLB) pitcher Tyler Skaggs resulted in a multiyear criminal court case, ending with the conviction of the team administrator who provided the drugs linked to Skaggs' death. Even as media coverage promised to reveal the "drug scourge in MLB clubhouses," both league statistics, and player interviews, deny a widespread opioid problem in the sport (Garcia-Roberts & Douglas, 2022). Indeed, despite the untimely deaths of several well-known sports stars in the past decade, statistics do not suggest catastrophic risk of harmful opioid use in sports, at any level.

At the same time, the athlete-opioid panic may also linger because, as Reinarman (1994, p. 159) has written of other drug scares, there exists a "kernel of truth," or "some basis to claim…there is a problem." Alas, as in other scares, this kernel is buried deep in the background, far from the headlines. On a superficial level, the misuse of opioids in sports appears unavoidable, if not preordained during a period in which POs were distributed without sufficient oversight. After all, athletes—casual and elite, young and old—are more prone to injury, and corrective surgery, than their nonathlete peers; moreover, sentinel surveillance shows that rates of sports-related surgery have risen persistently through the years, particularly among young people, as single-sport specialization and year-round leagues become more prevalent (Champion, 2021; Zaremski et al., 2019). For these reasons, one might expect more athlete exposure to drugs that carry the risk of physical, and psychological, dependence when used over long durations. Here, however, is where the previous four chapters may test the opioid-athletes narrative, highlighting a central flawed assumption: namely, that exposure begets misuse. Research reviewed in the following pages will reveal extraordinarily low rates of transition to nonmedical or illicit opioid use among individuals first prescribed pharmaceutical opioids for diagnosed ailments. Escalation or overconsumption of POs is far from inevitable within the general population, and perhaps even less likely among individuals whose athletic participation has been shown to shield them from most forms of substance use. Indeed, the bulk of scholarly studies have concluded sports involvement to function as a protective factor against nonmedical opioid use and dependence; the sport risk environment may, in fact, enable more controlled, less harmful patterns of opioid use, even as overarching population trends increase opioid consumption across the board.

And yet some longitudinal data has shown certain athlete demographics to suffer higher levels of harmful opioid use and related risks; the kernel of truth shines dimly, hidden in layers of culture, as the media focuses its attention on the drugs and their suppliers, not the broader context of consumption. While an "epidemic" may be hyperbolic, the conditions that enable rising nonmedical use within some sports and among some athletes are easily identified through the application of theories already reviewed in this text. In fact, they are cogently summarized in the *Sports Illustrated* article that opens this chapter: "As the sports industry expands each year—and the stakes on rinks, fields and courts grow higher—young athletes face enormous pressure to manage their pain and play through injuries" (Wertheim & Rodriguez, 2015). Even as little qualitative data exists on this topic, this chapter will explore the idea that the ethic of sport, increasingly exacerbated by a sociohistorical context that distributes disproportionate economic rewards for sporting success, may promote harmful patterns of opioid and other painkiller use among some athletes. It will also expand on research briefly referenced in Chapter 3 on the connection between image and performance-enhancing drugs (IPED) use and subsequent opioid initiation, a disputed pathway that points more to the structure of drug markets than the chemical properties of the substances themselves. Indeed, the elucidation of the "IPED gateway" sets up a culminating discussion of effective policy solutions to nonmedical opioid use among athletes. To date, there exists little research on evidence-based interventions for opioid dependence or opioid use disorder among athletes; however, a wealth of studies on opioids and other substances has concluded that supply reduction efforts to make drugs harder to access do not lessen associated harms. In fact, the opposite may be true, as shown in the preventable death of Tyler Skaggs and many more unknown athletes.

Athletes' Opioid Use During a Global Crisis: What Does the Research Say?

If scientific research on opioid use among athletes remains sparse, it nevertheless captures a broader cross section of athletes—by competition level and country—than those depicting alcohol consumption. Still, at the outset, it must be said that most studies are incapable of assessing the central question underlying this chapter: whether athletes are at elevated risk for the nonmedical use of prescription opioids (NUPO) (such as hydrocodone) or the consumption of illicit opioids (such as heroin). This is because the bulk of studies on this topic fails to measure opioid use within a comparison population of nonathletes, focusing instead on current or former sportspeople. Opioids, a class of drug characterized by their potent analgesic (pain-relieving) and sedative (relaxing and sleep-promoting) properties, are also not consistently disaggregated from other medicines or intoxicants consumed by athletes, limiting the relevance of several studies to the preceding query. Finally, many studies capture only prescribed opioid use and/or fail to disentangle medical versus nonmedical consumption. To review, the medical-nonmedical binary that is employed throughout this chapter references the sources through which individuals obtain opioids, as well as their adherence to consumption guidelines—not necessarily their motives for opioid use. "Medical use" describes the consumption of pharmaceutical opioids prescribed by a licensed health-care practitioner for a diagnosed disorder, at both the recommended dosage and with the suggested frequency. "Nonmedical use" encompasses all other consumption patterns, as well as the use of drugs procured outside of medical contexts, even if the purpose of consumption is pain management.

These distinctions are important, as few individuals who consume pharmaceutical opioids under and according to medical guidance continue using the drugs after their prescription has ended or transition to the use of illicit market opioids like heroin (Minozzi et al., 2013; Muhuri et al., 2013; Noble et al., 2010). Similarly, the harms associated with medical use of POs are very different than those that may follow nonmedical use or consumption of opioids obtained from informal or illegal sources. Where long-term use of POs for a chronic medical condition may result in physical dependence, and maladies such as persistent constipation, such side effects may be anticipated and managed to maintain patients' comfort. By contrast, the risks that may follow from taking POs in higher doses, or with greater frequency than advised, or sourcing opioid-type drugs with unknown origins, are far more unpredictable, and possibly deadly. Compared to other intoxicants, opioids, from morphine to hydrocodone and fentanyl, have a relatively slim therapeutic index, a measure of a drug's safety calculated by dividing its (average) lethal dose by its (average) effective dose (Prekupec et al., 2017). For this reason, opioids should be administered with careful attention to time and dosage, as overconsumption may lead to overdose (in the form of severe respiratory depression or failure). Obviously, when one is purchasing opioid pills, powders, or other substrates (such as "black tar" heroin) outside medical contexts, it is impossible to know how much of the desired opioid is contained therein—or what undesired substances are also included. It is precisely the unknown character of informally sourced opioids that heightens the risk of overdose and other toxicity; thus, policies that restrict individuals' medical access to opioids without treating physical or psychological dependence must be interrogated for unintended consequences.

Given the starkly different consequences of medical and nonmedical opioid use, it makes sense to catalog these two behaviors separately, while paying further attention to the particular kinds of opioids ingested, when such information is available. Table 1 catalogs a range of opioid-type substances cited in this chapter, as well as relative potencies calculated against morphine, the first opioid to be isolated from the poppy plant (*Papaver somniferum*). Research on the prevalence of medical opioid use among athletes displays a wide range of estimates, with percentages varying by competition level, sport, region, and year. A 2018 systematic review of pain-reliever (analgesic) use among elite athletes reports that, among 13 papers evaluated, nine found rates of prior opioid use to be under 1% (Harle et al., 2018). Other studies involving a variety of athletic populations found disparate levels of opioid consumption. A 2014 survey of 40 Italian cyclists found that 3.3% had consumed tramadol in the past three months, while a 1993 study of Nigerian professional athletes determined that 5.6% had used codeine in their lifetimes (Loraschi et al., 2014; Ohaeri et al., 1993). Alternative measures of opioid use prevalence have been employed by studies that report rates of drug dispensing, rather than athlete consumption. For example, researchers reported that, on average, South African athletes participating in the 2004 Olympics received 1.54 codeine-containing tablets during the games, and 4.4% of athletes competing at the 2000, 2004, 2008, and 2012 World Cup events were prescribed opioids (Derman, 2008; Pedrinelli et al., 2015). What can be gleaned from the foregoing numbers, all of which seek to represent levels of medical opioid ingestion among elite or professional athletes? Without measures of misuse and no "general population" reference rates offered, the meaning of such statistics is hard to gauge. A conservative assessment might opine that these prevalence rates—between <1% and 5.6%—appear quite low, while the health risk to any individual athlete is similarly modest, given their intense medical supervision. (A potential caveat, of course, is that that sociolegal risks of opioid use among elite athletes may be greater, if their consumption is not justified by a "therapeutic use exemption" accepted by doping authorities.)

Table 1: Relative Potencies of Commonly Used Opioids

Opioid Drug	Potency Relative to Morphine
Tramadol	1/10
Codeine	1/10
Hydrocodone	2/3
Morphine	n/a
Oxycodone	2
Diacetyl Morphine (Heroin)	2–3
Hydromorphone (Dilaudid)	4–5
Methadone	5–10
Buprenorphine (sublingual)	80
Fentanyl (transdermal)	100

(Source: European Monitoring Centre for Drugs and Drug Addiction (n.d.); World Health Organization (2018)

A handful of U.S. studies conducted among high school and college populations provide comparative statistics by athletic involvement, albeit with somewhat ambiguous results. Where a 2013 study of current U.S. college students showed that participants who had played at least one interscholastic sport in high school were 36% more likely to indicate lifetime medical use of POs, annual surveys conducted among middle and high school students between 2009 and 2012 found a similar effect size associated with "organized sports participation"—but only among male respondents (Veliz et al., 2014, 2015). The National Collegiate Athletic Association's (NCAA) quadrennial survey of college athletes' substance use does not compare medical consumption of "narcotic pain medications" against a control population of university students; however, this data may be held against other studies conducted in college-age populations. For example, in 2013, 15.7% of all students at a large state university reported past-year medical consumption of a prescription pain medication, compared to 18% of NCAA athletes that same year (McCabe et al., 2014; NCAA, 2014). Interestingly, a comparison of the NCAA sample to a general college population in 2009 yields a very different finding. While 16.5% of college respondents affirmed medical use of prescription painkillers in 2009, less than 15% of athletes indicated this behavior (McCabe et al., 2014; NCAA, 2014).

On balance, the medical use of POs appears more prevalent among lower-level athletes, specifically among U.S.-based school- and college-aged athletes. But does medical exposure translate to opioid misuse? Here, the data is far more contradictory, and nuanced, pointing to period, sex, and sport-specific effects. Looking at the impact of sports participation on nonmedical PO use in university athletes, three studies have arrived at different conclusions, albeit over different time periods. Using a nationally representative sample from 2001, Ford (2008) concluded that college student-athletes were categorically less likely than their nonathlete counterparts to have engaged in nonmedical prescription opioid use (NUPO) in their lifetime; yet Ford et al.'s (2018) analysis of past-year nonmedical opioid use by athletic status among participants sampled between 2008 and 2011 revealed the inverse association, with varsity athletes significantly more likely to report this behavior. Finally, Veliz et al.'s (2015) retrospective study of (college students') high school sports involvement and lifetime nonmedical opioid consumption found no relationship between these variables. Similarly, a 2017 analysis of NUPO and heroin among U.S. 12th graders showed no effects of athletic involvement, while a 2016 study of the same behaviors among 8th and 10th graders determined athletes to be at lower risk (Veliz et al., 2016, 2017). As noted previously, such muddled results may reflect temporal trends in PO use and misuse, with both possibly peaking in the early 2010s; in fact, the Centers for Disease Control affirms that opioid prescribing in the United States as a whole peaked in 2012 (CDC Injury Center, 2022a).

At the same time, a focus on the undifferentiated impact of athletic status on nonmedical opioid use may conceal important variations by athlete demographic and sport. Even as Ford et al. (2018) showed an overarching effect of sports involvement on nonmedical PO use, multivariate analysis demonstrated bifurcated effects for male and female college athletes. While NUPO was significantly higher among male athletes than nonathletes (11.5% vs. 9.2%), varsity sports involvement appeared to reduce the risk of this behavior for women, with only 7.4% of female athletes reporting past-year NUPO (vs. 7.7% of nonathletes). Importantly, Veliz et al. (2014) also isolated the influence of sex on nonmedical PO use among school age (7th–10th grade) athletes, with male sports participants more likely to indicate overconsumption of prescribed opioids, as well as use of the drugs to "get high." Two further variables, correlated with sex, have also been shown to be relevant to athletes' nonmedical opioid use. In Ford et al.'s (2018) study, the experience of a past-year injury elevated the rate of NUPO among all students, regardless of athletic status but appeared most salient among male athletes, whose rate of NUPO post injury was twice that of the general college population. Given the independent effects of sex and injury on NUPO risk, it is perhaps not surprising that certain male-dominated sports, characterized by high injury rates, have also shown associations with NUPO. Specifically, Veliz et al. (2013, 2017) identified increased odds of NUPO among individuals involved in (American) weightlifting, ice hockey, wrestling, and football, with participants in the latter two sports showing "nearly a 50% increase in the odds of [NUPO] compared with their peers who did not participate in these sports." (2017 NCAA data additionally highlights wrestling, ice hockey, and football among the top five male sports for use of narcotic pain medication.) The imbrication of sport, injury, and sex are explored in detail in a 2011 survey of former NFL players, which exposed devastating levels of nonmedical PO consumption among American football professionals, during and after their careers. Over half of players affirmed medical use of opioids while active, with 71% of this population participating in some form of nonmedical use. Moreover, 15% of retired athletes indicated ongoing or current NUPO, an outcome predicted by significant (injury-related) pain, undiagnosed concussions, and heavy drinking (Cottler et al., 2011).

Playing Through Pain? Theorizing the Narrow Opioid-Sport Nexus

The research reviewed previously consists almost entirely of survey studies of different athlete and student groups, with most conducting secondary analyses of data collected for a variety of purposes. Apart from basic participant demographics, sports and injury history, and prior drug use, there is little contextual data on the circumstances of athletes' medical and nonmedical opioid consumption. This is to say that while we may make some tentative conclusions about *how many* and *which* athletes are at heightened risk of harmful opioid use, we can only speculate as to *why* and *how* this risk is produced. While quantitative or statistical data is invaluable for determining the existence and scale of an epidemiological problem (such as nonmedical opioid use), qualitative evidence—generated from interviews, focus groups, or ethnography—is necessary to sketch the salient elements of risk environment and their interactions with individual psychology. In the absence of this rich data, however, we may sift through the theoretical frameworks presented in Chapter 3 and consider how they resonate with the predictors of NUPO seen here.

First, however, we might briefly theorize the negative associations found or implied by the majority of studies cited so far in this chapter: on the whole, athletes appear to engage in lower levels of nonmedical opioid use than their counterparts in the general population. The protective effect of sports involvement may even be muted, due to athletes' heightened exposure to injury and prescription pain medication. This statement contradicts much of what is commonly "known" about athletes' vulnerability to opioid dependence and associated harms, but is actually quite intuitive once we throw off the "pharmacological determinism" that shapes so many conversations around opioids (Reinarman & Levine, 1997). In other words, the behavioral effects of a psychoactive substance are not inherent in their chemical composition, nor do they derive immediately from their neuronal action in the brain. Instead, the short- and long-term impacts of ingestion reflect the interactions of drug, (mind)set, and setting, with the first element playing the slightest role (see Zinberg, 1986). As with several other popular intoxicants (such as alcohol, benzodiazepines, and nicotine), opioids are known to produce physiological dependence if consumed consistently, for an extended period; the sudden cessation of opioid use, in turn, may produce unpleasant withdrawal symptoms. These facts, taken in tandem with the pleasurable effects many individuals experience from opioids, have led to the inane truism that opioids are "instantly addictive," and thus harmful for anyone that is exposed. Of course, decades of data are available to puncture this mythology. Longitudinal data from vast annual studies in the United States and other countries indicates that less than 10% of individuals who have tried heroin, for example, report recent use of the drug (Center for Behavioral Health Statistics and Quality, 2021). The slide from the use of PO to that of illicit opioid is even rarer, with less than 4% of those who consume POs outside medical guidance initiating heroin (Muhuri et al., 2013). Other studies estimate that merely 0.6% of postoperative patients prescribed an opioid for pain go on to meet criteria for dependence or "abuse" or suffer an overdose (Brat et al., 2018).

Research within the general population thus tells us that nonmedical opioid use is rare, even among individuals who are "exposed" by a prescription. Why might athletes enjoy even higher rates of protection against harmful opioid use? Here, we might revert to Hirschi's (1969) theory of social control, which locates the avoidance of deviant or criminal behavior within individuals' stakes in conformity—the relationships and resources that they stand to lose if caught engaging in prohibited activities. This theory may be most relevant in explaining low rates of any opioid use among elite athletes, who are subject to regular surveillance and potentially career-ending sanctions. Opioid use outside of medical supervision—and more specifically, a therapeutic exemption—may result in competition disqualifications, team expulsions, dropped endorsements, and lost income. As the stigma around opioid use grows, the sports–social bond may become even more effective in the prevention of NUPO, as such behavior becomes a greater threat to one's participation and acceptance in athletic circles. Of course, social control theory is not "airtight"; some athletes at the highest levels will consume banned substances if they perceive that the advantages significantly outweigh the risks. Merton's strain theory may even be applicable here, when reflecting on the heavy use of opioids among NFL players described by Cottler et al. (2011); collectively, American football professionals are paid the most of any sport worldwide (Gaines, n.d.). Over the entirety of the sports landscape, however, this benefit–harm ratio may be much slimmer for drugs, such as opioids, without direct image- or performance-enhancing effects.

Even if athletes as a "class" are less vulnerable to NUPO, protection may be contingent on specific sport and team subcultures, which are sometimes known to be socially organized around substance use. The last chapter took up this idea in explaining high levels of harmful drinking among some college athletes, particularly males competing in team sports. University landscapes are, of course, awash in opportunities for alcohol consumption, and thus drinking represents an intuitive site of sociality for student-athletes seeking to celebrate a victory or bond post loss. Nevertheless, opioids represent another sedative-type drug, associated with relaxation in lower doses; depending on any one team's prescription environment, moreover, they may be similarly accessible. Sutherland's (1947) theory of differential association comes to mind here, in its emphasis on deviance, including drug use, as a behavior learned from close social contacts. Just as an athlete's history of injury has been shown to predict their subsequent involvement in NUPO, a team roster populated by injured players may see the spread of opioid use beyond individuals with legitimate prescriptions (Ford et al., 2018). Indeed, multiple studies have shown that those who use POs nonmedically typically source these substances from friends and family with medical access—not doctors (Inciardi et al., 2009; Jones et al., 2014). Research within university populations has additionally found that student-athletes with an opioid prescription are more likely to be approached for diversion of their medications (Veliz et al., 2015).

Finally, the learning of values supportive of NUPO may be easier among individuals already primed by the "ethic of sport." As discussed previously, this ethic may be toxic for some athletes, encouraging high-risk behaviors on and off the "field." Drug use that is understood to be in the service of sports success may be specifically sanctioned by athletes socialized in this ethic; in fact, Hughes and Coakley (1991), who first theorized the sports ethic, specifically considered IPED use as one outcome reflecting strict adherence to this social code. While opioids arguably do not boost performance, they certainly may facilitate playing through pain or injury—activities mandated by an ethic that advises "real" athletes to prioritize sports, ignore their physical limits, and seek success at all costs. Cottler et al.'s (2011) representation of past and present NUPO among retired NFL players is again salient here, which reveals that nonmedical opioid use was vastly increased among players with undiagnosed concussions. The authors speculate that such individuals decided to self-medicate their pain, fearing that "if they report a concussion, they will be pulled from active play." Hinting at the detrimental effects of the sports ethic as internalized by individuals at frequent risk of serious injury, Cottler et al.'s (2011) study also highlights the need for qualitative research that would not only draw out athletes' own narratives of NUPO but also outline the social infrastructure of harmful opioid use at the level of team or leagues. Anecdotal reports decry cultures of coercive doping or team-sponsored drug-dealing in some sports, but such evidence has not been revealed through systematic study. Cottler et al.'s (2011) survey nevertheless captured individuals who identified coaches, trainers, or "pill guys" as the source of their opioids, a reality that may be prevalent but remains undocumented.

Dope and Doping: Are IPEDs an Unchecked Gateway to Opioids?

A long-standing body of research indicates that individuals who use IPED also consume controlled psychoactive drugs such as cannabis, cocaine, and opioids (prescribed and illicit) at rates higher than those applicable to the general public. In other words, polysubstance use, and polypharmacy, may not be unusual in this population, which represents a diverse group of athletes (but includes a disproportionate share of strength and contact sports). For example, the most recent year of data from a longitudinal survey of IPED users in Wales, England, and Scotland found that 33% had consumed cannabis, 25% cocaine, and 1.4% heroin in the past year, while one in four had used prescription pain medication; within the overall adult population (aged 16 to 59), the same behaviors were markedly less common, reported by 6.6%, 2.3%, less than 0.1%, and 7.6% of individuals, respectively (Begley et al., 2017; Broadfield, n.d.). Similar disparities have been reported among individuals who consume IPED (for nonmedical purposes) in the United States and diverse European nations (see, for example, Denham, 2009; Dodge & Hoagland, 2011; DuRant et al., 1995; Kanayama et al., 2003; Kindlundh et al., 1999; Kokkevi et al., 2008; McCabe et al., 2007; Pallesen et al., 2006).

While these studies indicate that IPED (and predominantly, anabolic-androgenic steroids [AAS]) consumption is correlated with multiple forms of psychoactive, controlled substance use, correlation does not imply causation, nor does a mere statistical relationship tell us anything about individuals' sequence of substance use. In other words, data is needed about the order in which athletes initiated the use of IPED and other psychoactive substances, in order to determine whether the former functions as a "gateway." Moreover, we need to be able to formulate a plausible mechanism by which IPED may encourage subsequent experimentation with drugs that have markedly different effects than substances that are meant to promote muscular development, definition, and/or overall athletic performance. The gateway hypothesis, first proposed in 1975 to explain the uptake of "harder" illicit drugs (such as cocaine or heroin) after prior use of cannabis, has struggled to explain how this sequence operates, most recently arguing that cannabinoids biologically prime the brain to crave other kinds of drugs (Kandel, 1975; Kandel, 2003). While no similar research has suggested a similar neurochemical connection AAS and psychoactive substances, it should be stated that the former has no known pleasurable or intoxicating effects. (Indeed, such a statement applies to a majority of substances typically categorized as IPED, with the exception of ephedrine and other amphetamines, stimulants that also increase energy and metabolism.) Opioids, the category of psychoactive substances that form the focus of this chapter, have markedly different properties than any commonly used IPED, promoting sedation and relieving pain. Even if research evidence suggests that IPED consumption is often followed by opioid initiation, this relationship may have little to do with the pharmacology of the substances involved.

What does research tell us about drug use careers involving both IPED and opioids? On the one hand, the vast majority of research concerning polysubstance use among individuals who consume IPED is cross-sectional, capturing a single point in time, and thus cannot conclusively address questions of temporality. Moreover, all known studies in this area single out AAS as the IPEDs of interest, and the criterion used to identify "IPED users," a limitation that must temper any claims around the "IPED gateway." Still, a handful of projects have shown prior or current AAS use to shape different kinds of opioid initiation. The AAS-opioid "gateway" hypothesis was first stated in a 2000 letter to the *New England Journal of Medicine,* which reported that nearly 10% of individuals receiving treatment for opioid dependence at a private inpatient facility reported AAS use that predated their uptake of opioids (Arvary & Pope, 2000). While basing its claims on a small population of patients (21 men), the authors do propose several mechanisms linking AAS to heroin and other opioids. Among these twenty-one individuals, 86% initiated opioids for the purpose of managing negative side effects of AAS, 81% first purchased heroin from the same persons who sold AAS, 67% had been introduced to opioids by a fellow (bodybuilder) athlete, and 67% used opioids to cope with depression following AAS desistance. Similar motivations and structural pathways linking AAS and opioids have been characterized by later research. Most analogous is a 2015 study also conducted within a treatment population; one-quarter of men identifying opioids as their primary drug of dependence had a history of AAS use, while nearly 30% of interviewees reported that they had first learned about opioid at "the gym" and bought opioids and AAS from a single seller (Kanayama et al., 2003). Moreover, a clinical study of thirty-two individuals receiving treatment for AAS dependence in Sweden found that 25% had used heroin in their lifetimes, while 12.5% currently consumed the drug; interviews indicated that some of these patients had turned to heroin as a mean of "withdrawing" from AAS (Skarberg et al., 2009). Other studies have focused on the complementary effects of AAS and opioids, with individuals taking up opioids to improve sleep, maintain calm before competition, manage training-related pain, or continue training in the face of injury (Fudala et al., 2003; McBride et al., 1996). Finally, some studies have suggested that the injection of certain AAS may increase the likelihood of intravenous administration of heroin and other opioids (Larance et al., 2008; Wines et al., 1999).

It should also be noted that some cross-sectional studies reveal a reversed direction of AAS and opioid use, with Cornford et al. (2014), for example, showing that some individuals who use heroin strategically employ AAS as a means of gaining weight and alleviating the stigma associated with the former drug.

Considering dual use of AAS and heroin in Sweden, Garevik and Rane (2010) found that opioids typically preceded uptake of AAS among their participants. Evaluating the overall volume and types of data supporting this particular "gateway hypothesis," a causal relationship between AAS use and opioid initiation has not been definitively proven. Moreover, there is no evidence to suggest a biological or neurochemical relationship between AAS and subsequent opioid use (and indeed, this connection has only been tenuously sketched by studies on the effects of cannabis.) At the same time, the qualitative data characterizing trajectories of AAS and opioid use resonates with other research on sequences of illegal drug use, while providing an implicit critique of policies that prohibit and/or criminalize both image/performance-enhancing and psychoactive substances. Arguably, the speculative AAS-opioid gateway is a feature specific to the illicit markets where both substance types are traded. Since (nonmedical) AAS users must purchase these substances from informal vendors or "dealers," they are more likely to be exposed to other illicit products such individuals sell—for example, heroin or other opioids. Moreover, since their AAS consumption is not medically supervised, such users are left to their own devices when it comes to managing side effects, reduction, or desistance; in other words, opioids become an expedient means of self-medication within a "homespun" IPED regimen. In turn, we might infer that breaking the gateway might require dismantling the illegal marketplace—not by increasing the penalties associated with prohibition but by relocating AAS consumption to a legal, regulated space where risks can be proactively minimized. In moving to a concluding discussion of interventions to prevent harmful opioid use among athletes, we might do well to keep such considerations in mind, not least because recent efforts to restrict medical access to opioids have been followed by stark increases in illicit opioid use and overdose.

Evidence-Based Interventions for Opioid Use in Sports: Sketching a Blueprint

While there are few programs explicitly designed to address harmful drinking among athletes, there are no known interventions, at present, to prevent nonmedical opioid use, or treat opioid dependence, within sports in particular (Ekhtiari et al., 2020; Exner et al., 2021; Harle et al., 2018). The absence of specific programming may simply reflect the scale of the supposed problem: unsanctioned opioid use among athletes appears both minimal and in decline, although more recent research is required to validate this trend. As a reaction to the overdose crisis that has wracked North America and Australasia for over a decade, opioid prescribing has also declined in both regions, although the long-term consequences of this shift is unclear. Drug supply reduction is an endeavor historically complicated by unintended consequences, especially when unaccompanied by a simultaneous investment in prevention education, treatment, and harm reduction. Indeed, in the United States, efforts to sharply restrict medical access to pharmaceutical opioids through more stringent drug "scheduling," prescription drug monitoring programs, and the prosecution of suspect prescribers have had mixed results (Haynes et al., 2016; Kuo et al., 2018; Li et al., 2014; Martin et al., 2018; Raji et al., 2018; Usmani et al., 2021; Yang & Haffajee, 2016). On the one hand, pharmaceutical opioid dispensing has plummeted 50% since 2012, while deaths involving POs have plateaued (CDC Injury Center, 2022a). Over the same period, however, overdose mortality related to illicitly sourced opioids has skyrocketed, a surge that suggests that many individuals simply transitioned from controlled pharmaceuticals to their unregulated brethren (CDC Injury Center, 2022b). With many commentators attributing the rise of illicit opioid use, at least in part, to new limitations on PO availability, it is hard to assess the value of these new prohibitions (Powell & Pacula, 2020; Rhodes et al., 2019). In the context of a fractured, for-profit health-care system that neglects mental and behavioral health, most experts agree that excessive lassitude in opioid prescribing helped ignite the epidemic that continues to burn; comprehensive efforts to educate both prescribers and patients on the proper use of POs, and targeted crackdowns on bad-faith providers, were certainly justified. However, prohibition is a blunt tool that does not by itself realize the complexity of drug dependence. Expanded access to evidence-based care for opioid dependence—in short, demand reduction and harm reduction—must follow these supply constraints; unfortunately, such increases have not been even or sufficient (American Medical Association [AMA], n.d.).

What does evidence-based care for opioid dependence look like, and what effective forms of prevention exist around nonmedical opioid use at large? While not specific to athletes, there exists ample research to recommend specific demand and harm reduction interventions for opioid use, which may be adapted to the particular contours of the sports risk environment. Notably, a "gold standard" has long been recognized for the treatment of opioid use disorder, namely, medication-assisted treatment (MAT) using methadone or buprenorphine. Both synthetic opioids that adhere to the same brain receptors as heroin, oxycodone, or fentanyl, these two medications ameliorate cravings for and withdrawal from those shorter-acting drugs, allowing individuals to focus on other factors underlying their disorder (Fudala et al., 2003; Mattick et al., 2014; Schwartz et al., 2013; U.S. Department of Health and Human Services [HHS], Office of the Surgeon General, 2018). While internationally recognized as "essential medicines" by the WHO, both buprenorphine and methadone can be found on WADA's list of prohibited substances, whose sanctioned use would require a TUE (World Anti-Doping Agency [WADA], 2022). Even if (ultimately) permitted by the agency, this process raises thorny issues for would-be applicants. Opioid use disorder remains a widely stigmatized condition that elite athletes may be loathe to disclose to an organization founded on the detection and punishment of banned drug consumption. The criteria used to evaluate TUE requests, moreover, may not be wholly appropriate to a chronic behavioral health condition. "Therapeutic use," as defined by WADA, disqualifies a treatment regimen that "may produce any additional enhancement of performance beyond what might be anticipated by a return to the athlete's normal state of health," while guidelines stipulate that "there is no reasonable permitted therapeutic alternative" (WADA, 2022). Used to treat a chronic condition where relapse is expected, MAT may proceed over the course of months, years, or decades; there is no typical period for patients' return to a "normal state of health" (Center for Drug Evaluation and Research, 2019). Plenty of alternatives exist, but they are far less effective in preventing relapse, overdose, and other negative health outcomes.

Yet another substance banned by WADA has shown promise in reducing negative consequences related to opioid use, namely, through replacing both medical and nonmedical opioid consumption: cannabis. Increasingly legalized at the national and local levels for therapeutic purposes, cannabis represents a pain management alternative to opioids for athletes and nonathletes alike. At the state/regional level, medical cannabis has been associated with decreases in opioid prescribing, opioid hospitalizations, opioid-related traffic fatalities, and opioid overdose deaths (Bachhuber et al., 2014; Bradford & Bradford, 2016; Kim et al., 2016; Shi, 2017). Moreover, cannabis, used under medical supervision in conjunction with counseling, may itself represent an effective medicine for the treatment of opioid use disorder (Lucas, 2012). Most promising for athletes, recent research indicates that some cannabinoids have shown clinical efficacy in treating concussion-related pain—a finding with the potential to decouple the concussion–opioids connection discussed on the preceding pages (Cottler et al., 2011; McVige et al., 2018). In light of cannabis's therapeutic potential for injured athletes, as well as significant rates of nonmedical use, several professional sports leagues have sharply reduced or eliminated sanctions related to cannabis use (Docter et al., 2020; Kaplan, 2020). (In fact, U.S. Major League Baseball's agreement to remove cannabis from its list of "drugs of abuse" followed Tyler Skaggs' 2019 opioid overdose death.) These policy concessions are in line with elite athletes' realities of injury and stress management, as well as a culture of sport that exacerbates both. Pending significant changes to a system that not only encourages but also rewards bodily risk and victory at all costs, the liberalization of cannabis policies may represent a form of harm reduction within a complex risk environment.

Reflection Points

1. Why are many prescription opioids, including those used in the treatment of opioid use disorder, prohibited by antidoping organizations?

2. Do opioids represent image and performance-enhancing drugs (IPED)?

3. How might the liberalization of cannabis use in sport affect athletes' use of this and other psychoactive substances?

Glossary

Anabolic–Androgenic Steroids: A class of synthetic substances that promote muscular development, definition, and/or recovery. While AAS are sometimes consumed nonmedically by athletes for the purposes of enhancing strength, endurance, and recovery from injury, these drugs (which broadly mimic the naturally occurring testosterone) also have significant clinical use in the treatment of weight loss, muscular atrophy, and the treatment of hormonal disorders.

Gateway Hypothesis: A controversial theory of substance use proposing that marijuana use may encourage subsequent experimentation with other illicit drugs, including cocaine, heroin, and ecstasy.

Harm Reduction: A program or policy that seeks to minimize the negative consequences attached to certain contextually risky behaviors, without requiring abstinence from or cessation of that behavior. While the harm reduction concept originated in reference to illicit drug use, it has also been deployed within other stigmatized conditions and populations (e.g., tobacco use, commercial sex work)

Nonmedical Opioid Misuse: The consumption of opioid-type drugs that are not prescribed (to the individual consumer) and/or the consumption of prescribed opioids in ways that depart from medical guidance (e.g., use at a higher dosage or frequency or for the purposes of intoxication). Both legally- (e.g., oxycodone) and illegally manufactured (e.g., heroin) opioids may be consumed nonmedically.

Opioids: A class of substances that reduce the perception of pain, induce relaxation or sedation, and possibly cause euphoria. Opioids, such as morphine, oxycodone, heroin, and fentanyl, also produce physiological dependence, and withdrawal, when used consistently over an extended period of time.

Stigma: A negative label attached to certain conditions, traits, or behaviors, which may result in formal or informal social sanctions (e.g., mockery, ostracization, criminal justice involvement).

REFERENCES

American Medical Association. (n.d.). *Report shows decreases in opioid prescribing, increase in overdoses.* https://www.ama-assn.org/press-center/press-releases/report-shows-decreases-opioid-prescribing-increase-overdoses

Arvary, D., & Pope, H. G. (2000). Anabolic–androgenic steroids as a gateway to opioid dependence. *New England Journal of Medicine, 342*(20), 1532. https://doi.org/10.1056/NEJM200005183422018

Bachhuber, M. A., Saloner, B., Cunningham, C. O., & Barry, C. L. (2014). Medical cannabis laws and opioid analgesic overdose mortality in the United States, 1999–2010. *JAMA Internal Medicine, 174*(10), 1668–1673. https://doi.org/10.1001/jamainternmed.2014.4005

Begley, E., McVeigh, J., & Hope, V. (2017). *2016 National IPED info survey report.* Liverpool John Moores Universit. https://www.ipedinfo.co.uk/resources/downloads/2016%20National%20IPED%20Info%20Survey%20report%20FINAL.pdf

Bradford, A. C., & Bradford, W. D. (2016). Medical Marijuana laws reduce prescription medication use in medicare part D. *Health Affairs, 35*(7), 1230–1236. https://doi.org/10.1377/hlthaff.2015.1661

Brat, G. A., Agniel, D., Beam, A., Yorkgitis, B., Bicket, M., Homer, M., Fox, K. P., Knecht, D. B., McMahill-Walraven, C. N., Palmer, N., & Kohane, I. (2018). Postsurgical prescriptions for opioid naive patients and association with overdose and misuse: Retrospective cohort study. *BMJ*, *360*, j5790. https://doi.org/10.1136/bmj.j5790

Broadfield, D. (n.d.). *Drug misuse: Findings from the 2016/17 crime survey for England and Wales* (p. 44). Statistical Bulletins—Home Office Statistics under the National Statistics Code of Practice.

CDC Injury Center. (2022a, March 18). *U.S. opioid dispensing rate maps*. https://www.cdc.gov/drugoverdose/rxrate-maps/index.html

CDC Injury Center. (2022b, June 1). *Opioid data analysis and resources*. https://www.cdc.gov/opioids/data/analysis-resources.html

Center for Behavioral Health Statistics and Quality. (2021). *Results from the 2020 national survey on drug use and health: Detailed tables.* Substance Abuse and Mental Health Services Administration. https://www.samhsa.gov/data/

Center for Drug Evaluation and Research, U.S. Food & Drug Administration. (2019, April 18). *Information about Medication-Assisted Treatment (MAT)*. https://www.fda.gov/drugs/information-drug-class/information-about-medication-assisted-treatment-mat

Champion, C. (2021). Injuries among youth athletes are on the rise—But why? https://connect.uclahealth.org/2021/03/31/injuries-among-youth-athletes-are-on-the-rise-but-why/

Cornford, C. S., Kean, J., & Nash, A. (2014). Anabolic-androgenic steroids and heroin use: A qualitative study exploring the connection. *International Journal of Drug Policy*, *25*(5), 928–930. https://doi.org/10.1016/j.drugpo.2014.06.002

Cottler, L. B., Ben Abdallah, A., Cummings, S. M., Barr, J., Banks, R., & Forchheimer, R. (2011). Injury, pain, and prescription opioid use among former National Football League (NFL) players. *Drug and Alcohol Dependence*, *116*(1–3), 188–194. https://doi.org/10.1016/j.drugalcdep.2010.12.003s

Denham, B. E. (2009). Association between narcotic use and anabolic-androgenic steroid use among American adolescents. *Substance Use & Misuse*, *44*(14), 2043–2061. https://doi.org/10.3109/10826080902848749

Derman, W. E. (2008). Medication use by team South Africa during the XXVIIIth Olympiad: A model for quantity estimation for multi-coded team events. *South African Journal of Sports Medicine*, *20*(3), 7.

Docter, S., Khan, M., Gohal, C., Ravi, B., Bhandari, M., Gandhi, R., & Leroux, T. (2020). Cannabis use and sport: A systematic review. *Sports Health*, *12*(2), 189–199. https://doi.org/10.1177/1941738120901670

Dodge, T., & Hoagland, M. F. (2011). The use of anabolic androgenic steroids and polypharmacy: A review of the literature. *Drug and Alcohol Dependence*, *114*(2), 100–109. https://doi.org/10.1016/j.drugalcdep.2010.11.011

DuRant, R. H., Escobedo, L. G., & Heath, G. W. (1995). Anabolic-steroid use, strength training, and multiple drug use among adolescents in the United States. *Pediatrics*, *96*(1 Pt. 1), 23–28.

Ekhtiari, S., Yusuf, I., AlMakadma, Y., MacDonald, A., Leroux, T., & Khan, M. (2020). Opioid use in athletes: A systematic review. *Sports Health*, *12*(6), 534–539. https://doi.org/10.1177/1941738120933542

European Monitoring Centre for Drugs and Drug Addiction. (n.d.). *Heroin drug profile*. https://www.emcdda.europa.eu/publications/drug-profiles/heroin_en

Exner, J., Bitar, R., Berg, X., Pichler, E.-M., Herdener, M., Seifritz, E., & Claussen, M. C. (2021). Use of psychotropic substances among elite athletes—A narrative review. *Swiss Medical Weekly*. https://doi.org/10.4414/smw.2021.20412

Ford, J. A. (2008). Nonmedical prescription drug use among college students: A comparison between athletes and nonathletes. *Journal of American College Health*, *57*(2), 211–220. https://doi.org/10.3200/JACH.57.2.211-220

Ford, J. A., Pomykacz, C., Veliz, P., McCabe, S. E., & Boyd, C. J. (2018). Sports involvement, injury history, and non-medical use of prescription opioids among college students: An analysis with a national sample. *The American Journal on Addictions*, *27*(1), 15–22. https://doi.org/10.1111/ajad.12657

Fudala, P., Weinrieb, R., Calarco, J., Kampman, K., & Boardman, C. (2003). An evaluation of anabolic-androgenic steroid abusers over a period of 1 year: Seven case studies. *Annals of Clinical Psychiatry*, *15*(2), 121–130. https://doi.org/10.3109/10401230309085677

Gaines, C. (n.d.). *The NBA is the highest-paying sports league in the world*. Business Insider. https://www.businessinsider.com/sports-leagues-top-salaries-2015-5

Garcia-Roberts, G., & Douglas, J. (2022, February 22). MLB and opioids: Is this baseball's next drug scandal? *The Washington Post*. https://www.washingtonpost.com/sports/2022/02/22/mlb-opioid-epidemic-eric-kay-trial/

Garevik, N., & Rane, A. (2010). Dual use of anabolic-androgenic steroids and narcotics in Sweden. *Drug and Alcohol Dependence*, *109*(1–3), 144–146.

Government of Canada. (2022, March). *Opioid- and stimulant-related harms in Canada*. https://health-infobase.canada.ca/substance-related-harms/opioids-stimulants/

Harle, C. A., Danielson, E. C., Derman, W., Stuart, M., Dvorak, J., Smith, L., & Hainline, B. (2018). Analgesic management of pain in elite athletes: A systematic review. *Clinical Journal of Sport Medicine*, *28*(5), 417–426. https://doi.org/10.1097/JSM.0000000000000604

Haynes, A., Kleinschmidt, K., Forrester, M. B., & Young, A. (2016). Trends in analgesic exposures reported to Texas poison centers following increased regulation of hydrocodone. *Clinical Toxicology, 54*(5), 434–440. https://doi.org/10.3109/15563650.2016.1148720

Hirschi, T. (1969). *Causes of delinquency.* University of California Press.

Hughes, R., & Coakley, J. (1991). Positive deviance among athletes: The implications of overconformity to the sport ethic. *Sociology of Sport Journal, 8*(4), 307–325. https://doi.org/10.1123/ssj.8.4.307

Inciardi, J. A., Surratt, H. L., Cicero, T. J., Kurtz, S. P., Martin, S. S., & Parrino, M. W. (2009). The "black box" of prescription drug diversion. *Journal of Addictive Diseases, 28*(4), 332–347. https://doi.org/10.1080/10550880903182986

Jones, C. M., Paulozzi, L. J., & Mack, K. A. (2014). Sources of prescription opioid pain relievers by frequency of past-year nonmedical use: United States, 2008–2011. *JAMA Internal Medicine, 174*(5), 802–803. https://doi.org/10.1001/jamainternmed.2013.12809

Kaiser Family Foundation. (n.d.). *Opioid overdose deaths by age group.* https://www.kff.org/other/state-indicator/opioid-overdose-deaths-by-age-group/?currentTimeframe=0&sortModel=%7B%22colId%22:%22Location%22,%22sort%22:%22asc%22%7D

Kanayama, G., Cohane, G. H., Weiss, R. D., & Pope, H. G. (2003). Past anabolic-androgenic steroid use among men admitted for substance abuse treatment: An underrecognized problem? *The Journal of Clinical Psychiatry, 64*(2), 13902.

Kandel, D. (1975). Stages in adolescent involvement in drug use. *Science, 190*(4217), 912–914.

Kandel, D. B. (2003). Does Marijuana use cause the use of other drugs? *JAMA, 289*(4), 482–483. https://doi.org/10.1001/jama.289.4.482

Kaplan, E. (2020, April 30). *How weed became "whatever": Leagues are ditching old policies.* ESPN.Com. https://www

.espn.com/nfl/story/_/id/29114415/future-marijuana-drug-policy-nfl-pro-sports

Kim, J. H., Santaella-Tenorio, J., Mauro, C., Wrobel, J., Cerdà, M., Keyes, K. M., Hasin, D., Martins, S. S., & Li, G. (2016). State medical Marijuana laws and the prevalence of opioids detected among fatally injured drivers. *American Journal of Public Health*, *106*(11), 2032–2037. https://doi.org/10.2105/AJPH.2016.303426

Kindlundh, A. M. S., Isacson, D. G. L., Berglund, L., & Nyberg, F. (1999). Factors associated with adolescent use of doping agents: Anabolic-androgenic steroids. *Addiction*, *94*(4), 543–553. https://doi.org/10.1046/j.1360-0443.1999.9445439.x

Kokkevi, A., Fotiou, A., Chileva, A., Nociar, A., & Miller, P. (2008). Daily exercise and anabolic steroids use in adolescents: A cross-national European study. *Substance Use & Misuse*, *43*(14), 2053–2065. https://doi.org/10.1080/10826080802279342

Kuo, Y.-F., Raji, M. A., Liaw, V., Baillargeon, J., & Goodwin, J. S. (2018). Opioid prescriptions in older medicare beneficiaries after the 2014 federal rescheduling of hydrocodone products. *Journal of the American Geriatrics Society*, *66*(5), 945–953. https://doi.org/10.1111/jgs.15332

Larance, B., Degenhardt, L., Copeland, J., & Dillon, P. (2008). Injecting risk behaviour and related harm among men who use performance- and image-enhancing drugs. *Drug and Alcohol Review*, *27*(6), 679–686. https://doi.org/10.1080/09595230802392568

Li, G., Brady, J. E., Lang, B. H., Giglio, J., Wunsch, H., & DiMaggio, C. (2014). Prescription drug monitoring and drug overdose mortality. *Injury Epidemiology*, *1*(1), 9. https://doi.org/10.1186/2197-1714-1-9

Loraschi, A., Galli, N., & Cosentino, M. (2014). Dietary supplement and drug use and doping knowledge and att.... *Clinical Journal of Sport Medicine*, *24*(3), 238–244.

Lucas, P. (2012). Cannabis as an adjunct to or substitute for opiates in the treatment of chronic pain. *Journal of Psychoactive Drugs*, *44*, 125–133. https://doi.org/10.1080/02791072.2012.684624

Martin, J., Cunliffe, J., Décary-Hétu, D., & Aldridge, J. (2018). Effect of restricting the legal supply of prescription opioids on buying through online illicit marketplaces: Interrupted time series analysis. *BMJ*, *361*, k2270. https://doi.org/10.1136/bmj.k2270

Mattick, R. P., Breen, C., Kimber, J., & Davoli, M. (2014). Buprenorphine maintenance versus placebo or methadone maintenance for opioid dependence. *The Cochrane Database of Systematic Reviews*, *2*, CD002207. https://doi.org/10.1002/14651858.CD002207.pub4

McBride, A. J., Williamson, K., & Petersen, T. (1996). Three cases of nalbuphine hydrochloride dependence associated with anabolic steroid use. *British Journal of Sports Medicine*, *30*(1), 69–70. https://doi.org/10.1136/bjsm.30.1.69

McCabe, S. E., Brower, K. J., West, B. T., Nelson, T. F., & Wechsler, H. (2007). Trends in non-medical use of anabolic steroids by U.S. college students: Results from four national surveys. *Drug and Alcohol Dependence*, *90*(2–3), 243–251. https://doi.org/10.1016/j.drugalcdep.2007.04.004

McCabe, S. E., West, B. T., Teter, C. J., & Boyd, C. J. (2014). Trends in medical use, diversion, and nonmedical use of prescription medications among college students from 2003 to 2013: Connecting the dots. *Addictive Behaviors*, *39*(7), 1176–1182. https://doi.org/10.1016/j.addbeh.2014.03.008

McVige, J., Bargnes, V. H., Shukri, S., & Mechtler, L. (2018). Cannabis, concussion, and chronic pain: An ongoing retrospective analysis at Dent Neurologic Institute in Buffalo, NY. *Neurology*, *91*(23 Suppl. 1), S18–S19. https://doi.org/10.1212/01.wnl.0000550692.23055.1f

Minozzi, S., Amato, L., & Davoli, M. (2013). Development of dependence following treatment with opioid analgesics for pain relief: A systematic review. *Addiction*, *108*(4), 688–698. https://doi.org/10.1111/j.1360-0443.2012.04005.x

Muhuri, P., Gfroerer, J., & Davies, M. C. (2013). Associations of nonmedical pain reliever use and initiation of Heroin use in the United States. *CBHSQ Data Review*.

National Collegiate Athletic Association. (2014). *NCAA national study on substance use habits of college student-athletes.*

Noble, M., Treadwell, J. R., Tregear, S. J., Coates, V. H., Wiffen, P. J., Akafomo, C., & Schoelles, K. M. (2010). Long-term opioid management for chronic noncancer pain. *The Cochrane Database of Systematic Reviews*, *1*, CD006605. https://doi.org/10.1002/14651858.CD006605.pub2

Ohaeri, J. U., Ikpeme, E., Ikwuagwu, P. U., Zamani, A., & Odejide, O. A. (1993). Use and awareness of effects of anabolic steroids and psychoactive substances among a cohort of nigerian professional sports men and women. *Human Psychopharmacology: Clinical and Experimental*, *8*(6), 429–432. https://doi.org/10.1002/hup.470080609

Pallesen, S., Jøsendal, O., Johnsen, B.-H., Larsen, S., & Molde, H. (2006). Anabolic steroid use in high school students. *Substance Use & Misuse*, *41*(13), 1705–1717. https://doi.org/10.1080/10826080601006367

Pedrinelli, A., Ejnisman, L., Fagotti, L., Dvorak, J., & Tscholl, P. M. (2015). Medications and nutritional supplements in athletes during the 2000, 2004, 2008, and 2012 FIFA Futsal World Cups. *BioMed Research International*, *2015*, 1–6. https://doi.org/10.1155/2015/870308

Powell, D., & Pacula, R. L. (2020). The evolving consequences of OxyContin reformulation on drug overdoses. *American Journal of Health Economics*, *7*, 41–67.

Prekupec, M. P., Mansky, P. A., & Baumann, M. H. (2017). Misuse of novel synthetic opioids: A deadly new trend. *Journal of Addiction Medicine*, *11*(4), 256–265. https://doi.org/10.1097/ADM.0000000000000324

Raji, M. A., Kuo, Y.-F., Adhikari, D., Baillargeon, J., & Goodwin, J. S. (2018). Decline in opioid prescribing after federal rescheduling of hydrocodone products. *Pharmacoepidemiology and Drug Safety*, *27*(5), 513–519. https://doi.org/10.1002/pds.4376

Reinarman, C. (1994). The social construction of drug scares. In *Constructions of deviance: Social power, context, and interaction* (pp. 92–104). Wadsworth Publishing.

Reinarman, C., & Levine, H. (Eds.). (1997). *Crack in America: Demon drugs and social justice*. University of California Press.

Rhodes, E., Wilson, M., Robinson, A., Hayden, J. A., & Asbridge, M. (2019). The effectiveness of prescription drug monitoring programs at reducing opioid-related harms and consequences: A systematic review. *BMC Health Services Research, 19*(1), 784. https://doi.org/10.1186/s12913-019-4642-8

Schwartz, R. P., Gryczynski, J., O'Grady, K. E., Sharfstein, J. M., Warren, G., Olsen, Y., Mitchell, S. G., & Jaffe, J. H. (2013). Opioid agonist treatments and heroin overdose deaths in Baltimore, Maryland, 1995–2009. *American Journal of Public Health, 103*(5), 917–922. https://doi.org/10.2105/AJPH.2012.301049

Shi, Y. (2017). Medical Marijuana policies and hospitalizations related to Marijuana and Opioid pain reliever. *Drug & Alcohol Dependence, 173*, 144–150.

Skarberg, K., Nyberg, F., & Engstrom, I. (2009). Multisubstance use as a feature of addiction to anabolic-androgenic steroids. *European Addiction Research, 15*(2), 99–106.

Sutherland, E. (1947). Differential association. *Journal of Psychiatry, 102*, 674–682.

U.S. Department of Health and Human Services, Office of the Surgeon General. (2018). *Facing addiction in America: The surgeon general's spotlight on opioids*. https://addiction.surgeongeneral.gov/sites/default/files/Spotlight-on-Opioids_09192018.pdf

Usmani, S. A., Hollmann, J., Goodin, A., Hincapie-Castillo, J. M., Adkins, L. E., Ourhaan, N., Oueini, R., Bhagwandass, H., Easey, T., & Vouri, S. M. (2021). Effects of hydrocodone rescheduling on opioid use outcomes: A systematic review. *Journal of the American Pharmacists Association, 61*(2), e20–e44. https://doi.org/10.1016/j.japh.2020.09.013

Veliz, P. T., Boyd, C., & McCabe, S. E. (2013). Playing through pain: Sports participation and nonmedical use of opioid medications among adolescents. *American Journal of Public Health*, *103*(5), e28–e30. https://doi.org/10.2105/AJPH.2013.301242

Veliz, P., Boyd, C. J., & McCabe, S. E. (2016). Nonmedical prescription Opioid and Heroin use among adolescents who engage in sports and exercise. *Pediatrics*, *138*(2), e20160677. https://doi.org/10.1542/peds.2016-0677

Veliz, P., Boyd, C. J., & McCabe, S. E. (2017). Nonmedical use of prescription opioids and Heroin use among adolescents involved in competitive sports. *Journal of Adolescent Health*, *60*(3), 346–349. https://doi.org/10.1016/j.jadohealth.2016.09.021

Veliz, P., Epstein-Ngo, Q., Austic, E., Boyd, C., & McCabe, S. E. (2015). Opioid use among interscholastic sports participants: An exploratory study from a sample of college students. *Research Quarterly for Exercise and Sport*, *86*(2), 205–211. https://doi.org/10.1080/02701367.2014.983219

Veliz, P., Epstein-Ngo, Q. M., Meier, E., Ross-Durow, P. L., McCabe, S. E., & Boyd, C. J. (2014). Painfully obvious: A longitudinal examination of medical use and misuse of opioid medication among adolescent sports participants. *Journal of Adolescent Health*, *54*(3), 333–340. https://doi.org/10.1016/j.jadohealth.2013.09.002

Wertheim, L. J., & Rodriguez, K. (2015). *Special report: How painkillers are turning young athletes into Heroin addicts*. Sports Illustrated. https://www.si.com/more-sports/2015/06/18/special-report-painkillers-young-athletes-heroin-addicts

Wines, J. D., Jr., Gruber, A. J., Pope H. G., Jr., & Lukas, S. E. (1999). Nalbuphine Hydrochloride dependence in anabolic steroid users. *The American Journal on Addictions*, *8*(2), 161–164. https://doi.org/10.1080/105504999305965

World Anti-Doping Agency. (2022). *2022 List of prohibited substances and methods*. https://www.wada-ama.org/en/resources/world-anti-doping-program/prohibited-list

World Health Organization. (2018). *WHO guidelines for the pharmacological and Radiotherapeutic management of cancer pain in adults and adolescents.* [Text]. https://www.ncbi.nlm.nih.gov/books/NBK537482/table/appannex6.tab2/

Yang, Y. T., & Haffajee, R. L. (2016). When do opioid prescribers become criminals? *Mayo Clinic Proceedings*, *91*(10), 1331–1335. https://doi.org/10.1016/j.mayocp.2016.06.018

Zaremski, J. L., Zeppieri, G., & Tripp, B. L. (2019). Sport specialization and overuse injuries in adolescent throwing athletes: A narrative review. *Journal of Athletic Training*, *54*(10), 1030–1039. https://doi.org/10.4085/1062-6050-333-18

Zinberg, N. (1986). *Drug, set, and setting: The basis for controlled intoxicant use*. Yale University Press.

CHAPTER 6

Conclusion

Main Takeaways: An Unjustified "War on (Psychoactive) Drugs" in Sport

Having reviewed a disparate, but still slim, body of research on psychoactive substance use among athletes at all levels, this book must propose one primary takeaway: compared to similarly aged individuals in the general population, athletes appear to engage in relatively low levels of drug use. Socialized by a media sphere that foregrounds celebrity scandals, this summation may surprise anyone who has not read the preceding pages; however, both decades of data and established social theories support and clarify this conclusion. Where "hard" drug testing data reveals scant evidence of any illicit drug use among elite athletes competing on the global stage, myriad self-report studies conducted in professional and school-level sports overwhelmingly show the same. While still "human," to recall Sha'Carri Richardon's poignant explanation, athletes on the whole appear less amenable to the appeal of psychoactive drugs, at least during their active careers. Of course, this data is replete with gaps and methodological limitations. Drug testing is sporadic, restricted to controlled substances, and, arguably, incentivizes evasion. Similarly, self-disclosure studies of any stigmatized behaviors are bound to suffer from bias. Still, evaluated as a whole, the literature coalesces around the "low-risk" hypothesis. It also resonates with social theories that would suggest the protective effect of sport participation. As a conventional social institution, sport encourages compliance with informal norms and formal laws, at the risk of ostracization or expulsion. Sport may also represent a close-knit social milieu, from which individuals draw their closest friends and behavioral references. Finally, sport is still seen as an equal-opportunity pathway to socioeconomic success, albeit one that requires extreme physical and social discipline. While outside the scope of this text, emerging research also suggests that the physiological effects of regular exercise may deter individuals from drug-use initiation and even prevent relapse among those in recovery from a SUD (Swenson et al., 2020).

This general conclusion around psychoactive drug use and sport is not without its caveats. As previous chapters have also shown, certain sports, and athlete demographics, are associated with higher levels of some kinds of substance use. If we locate the protective effect of athletic involvement in the unique social relationships, commitments, and aspirations offered by different sports and teams, we might not be surprised by these inconsistencies; after all, "sport" is not a homogeneous social environment but rather one that varies vastly by location, level, activity, and demographic. In other words, an adolescent female football player in Chile is navigating a much different "drug ecosystem" than a professional male rugby player in New Zealand. Indeed, this is perfectly in keeping with the theory of risk environments, which not only deconstructs specific social contexts (such as sport) into different sites of risk production (and reduction) but further posits the interaction of micro- (e.g., team, league) and macro-level (e.g., national, global legal) environments. Focusing solely on substances with psychoactive effects, risk environment and related theories illuminate the increased, and sometimes excessive, use of one drug among some athlete subcultures: alcohol. As discussed in Chapter 4, drinking may represent a social ritual that bonds (largely male, team-sport) athletes, while demonstrating their adherence to the culture of sport, a code that rewards extreme physical behaviors and risk-taking; it is also a form of drug use that is normative within many cultures of the Global North, consonant with banned substance protocols, and widely commercialized in the sports entertainment arena. Less evidence supports the hypothesis of widespread opioid misuse among athletes, although elements of the risk environment offer a plausible theory for this problem. Under increasing pressure to succeed in sport from a young age, athletes may access potent, legal medications to "play through pain" during injuries or after surgeries. Known to quickly promote physical dependence after regular use, these drugs may remain, and provide comfort, long after sports careers end. Although this narrative has not been shown to characterize a significant population of athletes, we might remain attentive to the risks of opioid misuse in sports at all competition levels, as a global opioid epidemic continues to accelerate and elements of the sport risk environment propel success at all costs.

A relatively constant feature of the sport risk environment at the elite level of competition is a punitive regime of drug prohibition, enforced through testing and sanctions. In combination with a winner-takes-all system of monetary and symbolic rewards, this zero-tolerance approach to substance use among high-performance athletes may perversely promote more harmful forms of drug consumption within a population otherwise at low risk of initiation. On the one hand, seamless surveillance of drug consumption is logistically impossible, resulting in an inevitably spotty system that punishes an unlucky few; the inherent gaps within the test-sanction system may also empower some individuals to experiment with banned substances (image- and performance-enhancing, psychoactive, or both), if the benefits are perceived as eclipsing uncertain costs. Indeed, this points to the primary biomedical risks of drug prohibition in sport. While failing to eliminate banned drug use, a system founded on the threat of punishment incentivizes the unsupervised, clandestine consumption of informally sourced (and/or novel, less known) substances. Stated another way, drug prohibition in sport forces athletes to be "innovators," pioneering new ways of taking new drugs at their own risk (Merton, 1938). This is not to say that such individuals are cavalier about potential harms to their health; rather, they may prioritize avoidance of the social, legal, and career sanctions associated with an adverse test finding. (Studies have additionally shown that the consumption of banned substances may be more common among athletes in more precarious career positions, struggling to maintain their place on an elite team [Aubel & Ohl, 2014]). While some may argue that the extremely low percentages of positive test results reported by WADA are evidence of this system's success, we might consider the persistent discrepancies between self-report and drug testing data as revealing the "dark figure" of drug use in elite sport, even as more continuous methods of surveillance (such as the Athlete Biological Passport) continue to be rolled out (see, for example, Striegel et al., 2010). Even if this figure is not high, it represents missed opportunities to equip athletes with evidence-based information on how to manage their substance use in ways that benefit their health and livelihood. Moreover, testing data certainly fails to capture the presence of novel substances or existing drug analogs, the appeal of which lie in their ability to elude testing – even if their benefits or side effects are uncertain. Finally, we might recall the hypothesized IPED "gateway" (even if its contours remain blurry): athletes who are determined to access prohibited substances for image or performance enhancement may in turn encounter illegal psychoactive substances in the same marketplace, an exposure not without risks.

Societal Relevance: Sport as a Microcosm of Larger Drug Use Trends

To restate and summarize this text's major conclusions, one might say that psychoactive drug use in sport is a socially constructed problem; as a relatively rare phenomenon, it has become a site of public concern through persistent moral entrepreneurship and media magnification, a problem buoyed by its resonance with other cultural narratives around the spirit of sport, the moral value of temperance, and the perils of celebrity (among others) (Becker, 1997). Athletes' substance use, however, is also socially constructed in the sense that it is shaped by its social context, writ small and large. This is to say that despite the protective effect of sport, athletes' psychoactive substance use is subject to the same structural factors that shape drug use in the general population. Several examples discussed in this text illustrate this point. Even while the "opioid crisis" among athletes may have been overstated, athletes likely experienced increases in opioid exposure in the first 15 years of the millennium, a period in which POs were less regulated. The sport-specific risk environment was shaped by changes in global drug markets, national drug policies, and medical knowledge around pain, even as drug-use deterrent features of this environment served to moderate potential harms for athletes. For other drugs, the sports environment may have maintained, or ratcheted up, the risks faced by athlete consumers. University enrollment is a well-known risk factor for binge and heavy drinking among young adults, and while student populations have posted overall declines in harmful alcohol use over the past decade, some athletes continue to outdrink their peers through the present. When it comes to alcohol overconsumption in higher education, student-athletes are no exception—in fact, they may prove the rule. In this nested context, athletes may drink to alleviate the concurrent stresses of school and sport or to solidify new social bonds with not only their classmates but also their teammates; heavy alcohol use may also function as a means of establishing their dual identity as student-athletes.

A key element of the macro-level risk environment, national drug policies and laws, may affect athletes in complex ways. First, new societal-level drug prohibitions are quickly reflected in an expanded list of banned substances monitored by antidoping authorities. For example, in 2014, WADA added cathinone, and its synthetic derivatives, including mephedrone, to its prohibited list (Sallam et al., 2016). A class of stimulants deriving from (or mimicking) the khat plant, cathinones achieved infamy in the United Kingdom and the United States in the early 2010s as drugs favored by clubgoers, self-harming teenagers, and "cannibals" (ABC News, 2012; Shepherd, 2014). While no epidemiological evidence revealed the widespread use of cathinones—better known colloquially as "meow" or "bath salts"—among athletes, or the general population, the United States and Canada classified the drugs as "Schedule 1" substances in 2012, with WADA shortly following suit. At the same time, antidoping authorities may be slow to adapt to the liberalization of substance use laws at the national or state level. While WADA removed cannabidiol, a cannabis derivative with only mild psychoactive properties, from its list in 2017, THC remains prohibited, despite a global wave of laws decriminalizing and/or legalizing the drug. For some athletes, the inconsistency of governmental laws and sports-authority policies has amounted to a career-stalling trap; to recall a case widely referenced in this book, U.S. sprinter Sha'Carri Richardson lost her berth at the 2021 Tokyo Olympics after smoking cannabis in a state (Oregon) where the drug has been legal since 2015 (Jones, 2021). To date, many prominent athletes have characterized the discrepancy between drug laws and doping policies as unfair, while also alleging a problem well documented within society at large: Black athletes, and Black female athletes, in particular, are more vulnerable to scrutiny around their success, bodies, and (suspected) substance use (Herrington, 2021). Such scrutiny is seen as particularly pernicious when it sanctions the use of marijuana, a drug prohibited by WADA for ambiguous reasons. Even as multiple professional leagues have formally acknowledged the effectiveness of medical cannabis for pain management, this acceptance has not been extended to elite "amateur" athletes whose careers are the most precarious. In an effort to cajole reform in antidoping policies, some athletes have compared the relatively modest harms associated with cannabis use to those implied by POs—a favorable risk assessment that has been documented in the scholarly literature (Hsu & Kovács, 2021; Kim et al., 2016; Shi, 2017).

Links to Other Topics: Further Reading

As repeated ad nauseum throughout this text, sport is not a hermetically sealed social environment but one that is constantly reshaped by society at all levels (in different ways, depending on the local and national context). Moreover, athletes maintain multiple identities and social roles, formed through life experiences that are hardly standardized. At the end of the day, psychoactive drug use in sport inevitably exceeds the influence of a single institution, as a complex behavior reflecting an assemblage of social, psychological, and biological factors. To focus on the social influences that have dominated this book, we must reiterate that drug use among athletes cannot be fully grasped apart from psychoactive substance use in the population at large. To understand and predict trends in athlete drug use, one would be well served to stay abreast of the global epidemiology of substance use at large. The annual World Drug Report, released by the United Nations Office on Drugs and Crime, is an excellent resource for data on global drug use and market dynamics, which additionally addresses global events of cross-cutting import (such as the COVID-19 pandemic). The yearly publication additionally illuminates region- and nation-specific trends that may reflect unique geographic, cultural, policy, or demographic circumstances. In 2021, the Report highlighted global increases in the consumption of nonmedical cannabis and sedative-type drugs, a rapid expansion of online "cryptomarkets" for illicit drugs, as well as a predicted surge of substance use in Africa in the coming decade (in line with demographic trends) (United Nations Office on Drugs and Crime, 2021). All of these developments may translate from the world stage to the sports arena, in ways that can be expected to affect, and be affected by, drug and antidoping policies.

In fact, to comprehend athletes', and others', drug use, we must hone a critical knowledge of drug policy—a statement that may surprise those who assume drug laws flow from and reflect actual problems in consumption. It is the contention of this text that drug laws may foster or severely exacerbate the problems they are meant to solve, in pushing individual consumers to experiment with new or less known substances in clandestine ways. We should also recognize that prohibition, in sport or in society, more generally, may produce the first "hard evidence" of a newly banned substance, in the form of arrests, positive tests, or emergency room mentions. By first naming and then actively looking for problematic substances, prohibition policies and laws may be self-justifying by design. For this reason, one might maintain a healthy skepticism when processing data on a newly banned substance and additionally interrogate new bans for their resonance with drug laws at a larger scale. For that matter, individuals interested in the uneven evolution of drug policies in sport and outside might keep an eye on the (re)medicalization of a growing list of psychedelic drugs in North America, Europe, and Australasia. With substances such as methylenedioxymethamphetamine (MDMA) and psilocybin increasingly investigated for their applications to posttraumatic stress, eating, and SUD, additional "showdowns" between national drug and international doping policies may be imminent.

This leads us to a final site of vital connections for those interested in psychoactive substance use among athletes, namely IPED and doping. As discussed in the introduction, the boundaries between psychoactive and "image and performance enhancing" drugs are blurry at best. Drugs in (and spanning) each category are included within WADA's prohibited list, as well as national-level prohibition statutes. Substances determined to improve performance may also have psychoactive properties, and, indeed, consumers may be primarily, if not solely, interested in their intoxicating effects. Considering the enforcement of antidoping policies, motivation is largely irrelevant, if an individual has not received a therapeutic use exemption (TUE). The hypothesized "IPED gateway" is perhaps an artifact of a system that claims to differentiate IPED from other drug use, while punishing them similarly. With both types of substance restricted and sanctioned, individuals seeking anabolic-androgenic steroids (AAS) may be offered the purchase of other illicit drugs (which may, in turn, manage the side effects of unsupervised AAS use). While it is perhaps impossible to create static categories of substances that do/do not improve image and performance, the linkages between IPED and psychoactive drugs are socially forged by statutes that stigmatize them similarly. Ultimately, these distinctions may simply be convenient; the accusation of image or performance enhancement may provide an easy way to discredit athletes who are only pursuing basic human experiences: relaxation, pleasure, and a release from the stresses of a taxing career.

Reflection Points

1. How can research demonstrating the protective effect of sport against psychoactive substance use be applied more generally? Can protective elements of the sport environment be extended to nonathlete populations?

2. How might global trends toward the liberalization of marijuana laws affect antidoping policies and their prohibition of different psychoactive drugs in the long term?

3. How might antidoping and sport-specific drug policies best promote athlete health and safety?

REFERENCES

ABC News. (2012, June 1). Face-eating cannibal attack may be latest in string of "bath salts" incidents. *ABC News*. https://abcnews.go.com/Blotter/face-eating-cannibal-attack-latest-bath-salts-incident/story?id=16470389

Aubel, O., & Ohl, F. (2014). An alternative approach to the prevention of doping in cycling. *International Journal of Drug Policy*, *25*(6), 1094–1102. https://doi.org/10.1016/j.drugpo.2014.08.010

Becker, H. S. (1997). *Outsiders: Studies in sociology of deviance*. Free.

Herrington, A. J. (2021). *Cannabis takes the world stage at the Tokyo Olympics*. Forbes. https://www.forbes.com/sites/ajherrington/2021/07/21/cannabis-takes-the-world-stage-at-the-tokyo-olympics/

Hsu, G., & Kovács, B. (2021). Association between county level cannabis dispensary counts and opioid related mortality rates in the United States: Panel data study. *BMJ*, *372*. https://doi.org/10.1136/bmj.m4957

Jones, C. (2021, July 9). Why can't Olympians smoke weed? *PBS NewsHour*. https://www.pbs.org/newshour/nation/why-cant-olympians-smoke-weed

Kim, J. H., Santaella-Tenorio, J., Mauro, C., Wrobel, J., Cerdà, M., Keyes, K. M., Hasin, D., Martins, S. S., & Li, G. (2016). State medical marijuana laws and the prevalence of opioids detected among fatally injured drivers. *American Journal of Public Health*, *106*(11), 2032–2037. https://doi.org/10.2105/AJPH.2016.303426

Merton, R. K. (1938). Social structure and anomie. *American Sociological Review*, *3*(5), 672–682. https://doi.org/10.2307/2084686

Sallam, M. A., Sheikh, K. A., Baxendale, R., Azam, M. N., & El-Setouhy, M. (2016). The physiological and perceptual effects of plant extracts (Catha Edulis Forsk) during sustained exercise. *Substance Abuse Treatment, Prevention, and Policy*, *11*. https://doi.org/10.1186/s13011-016-0063-4

Shepherd, J. E. (2014, January 17). New drug alert: What is meow? *Rolling Stone*. https://www.rollingstone.com/culture/culture-news/what-is-meow-meow-the-drug-that-made-a-teen-cut-off-his-genitals-51319/

Shi, Y. (2017). Medical marijuana policies and hospitalizations related to marijuana and opioid pain reliever. *Drug & Alcohol Dependence*, *173*, 144–150. https://doi.org/10.1016/j.drugalcdep.2017.01.006.

Striegel, H., Ulrich, R., & Simon, P. (2010). Randomized response estimates for doping and illicit drug use in elite athletes. *Drug and Alcohol Dependence*, *106*(2), 230–232. https://doi.org/10.1016/j.drugalcdep.2009.07.026

Swenson, S., Blum, K., McLaughlin, T., Gold, M. S., & Thanos, P. K. (2020). The therapeutic potential of exercise for neuropsychiatric diseases: A review. *Journal of the Neurological Sciences*, *412*, 116763. https://doi.org/10.1016/j.jns.2020.116763

United Nations Office on Drugs and Crime. (2021). *World drug report 2021*. United Nations.

www.ingramcontent.com/pod-product-compliance
Lightning Source LLC
Chambersburg PA
CBHW032154160426
43197CB00008B/902